TWENTY-FOUR-HOUR BOOK SERIES

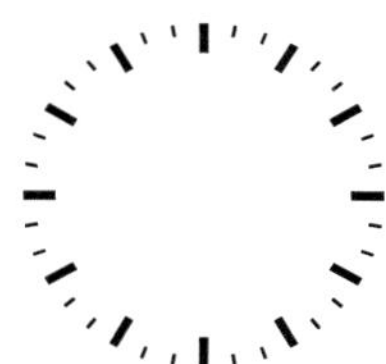

CABINET BOOKS, NEW YORK

Inspired by literary precedents such as automatic writing, by the resourcefulness of the *bricoleur* making do with what is at hand, and by the openness toward chance that all artistic production under severe constraint must necessarily incorporate, Cabinet's "24-Hour Book" series invites a number of distinguished authors and artists to be incarcerated in its gallery space to complete a project from start to finish within twenty-four hours.

Drawn between 10:00 am, 14 May 2016
and 10:00 am, 15 May 2016

Hail, Cretin!
David Scher

No. 2 in Cabinet's "24-Hour Book" series

For Melby and Rachel

David Scher is an artist living in New York City. He is represented by Pierogi in New York, Galerie Jean Brolly in Paris, and Galerie Ute Parduhn in Dusseldorf. In 1969, he cofounded o.n.e.m., a performance and music group that has persisted.

David Scher at his temporary desk at Cabinet making *Hail, Cretin!*. Photo taken at 5:23 AM on Sunday, 15 May 2016.

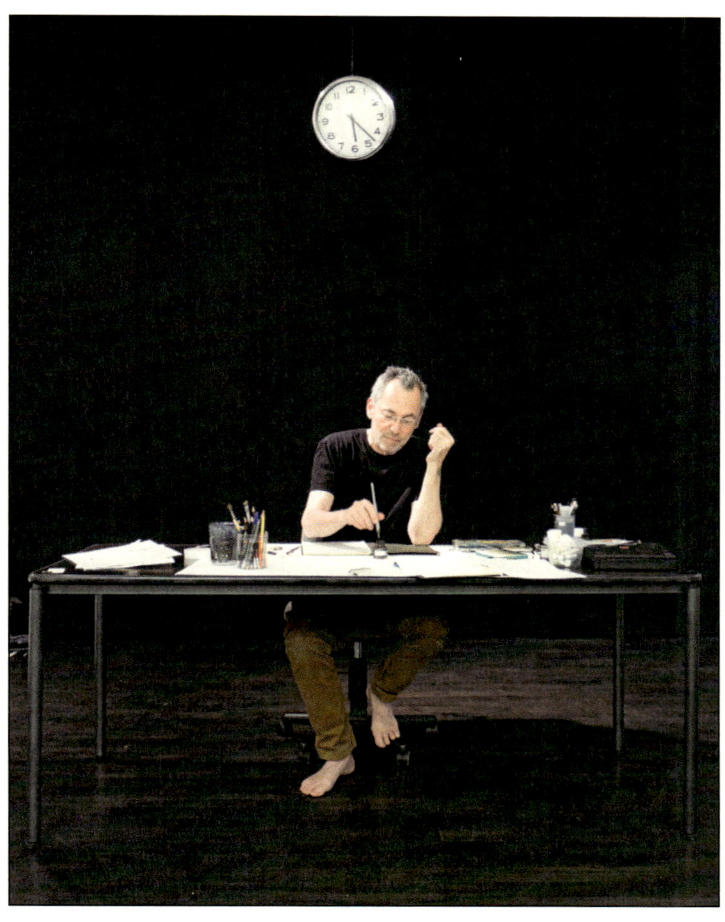

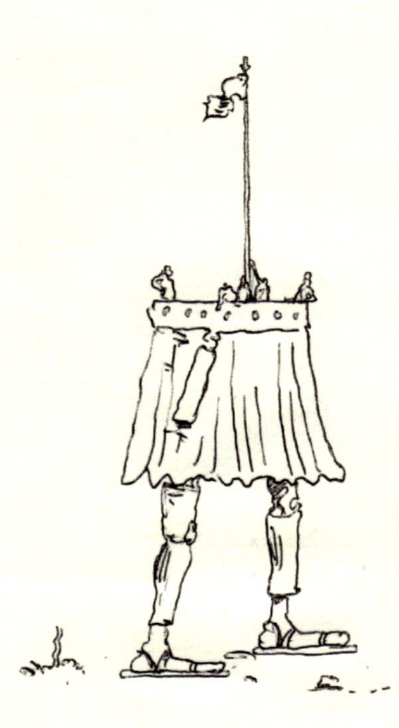

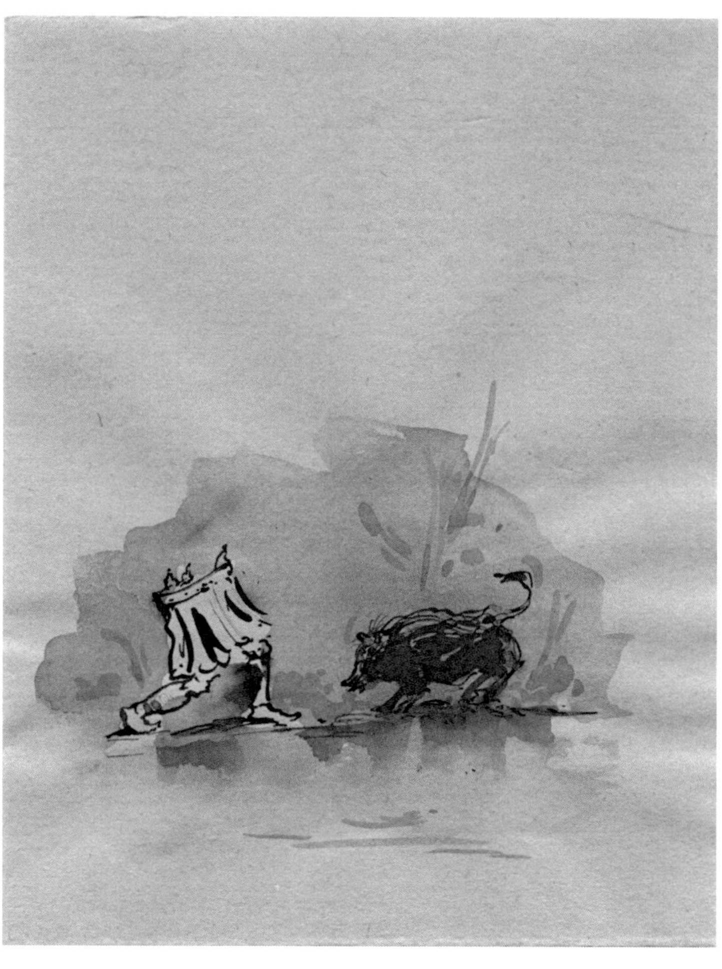

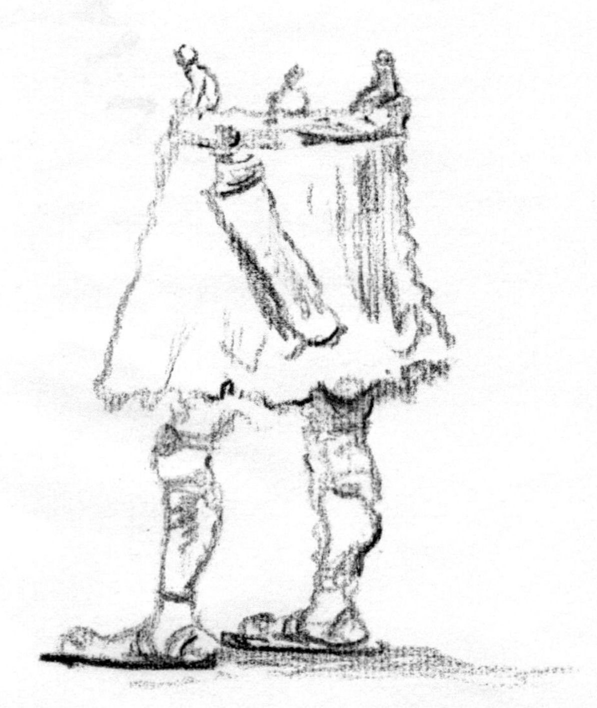

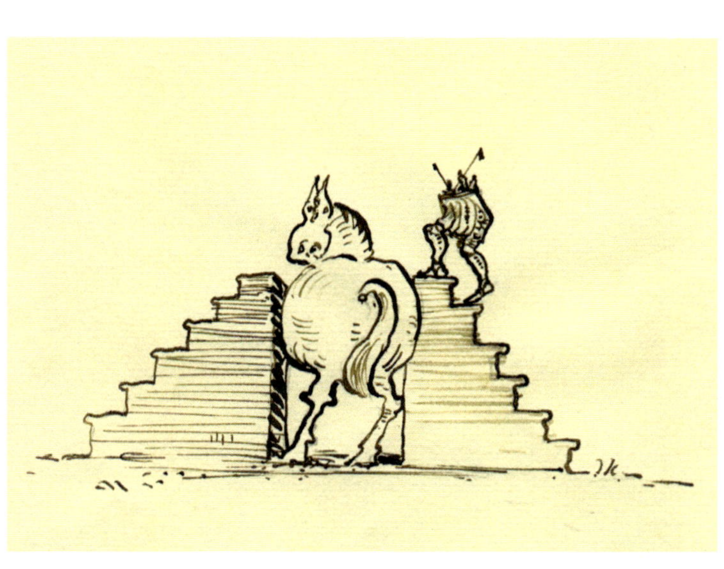

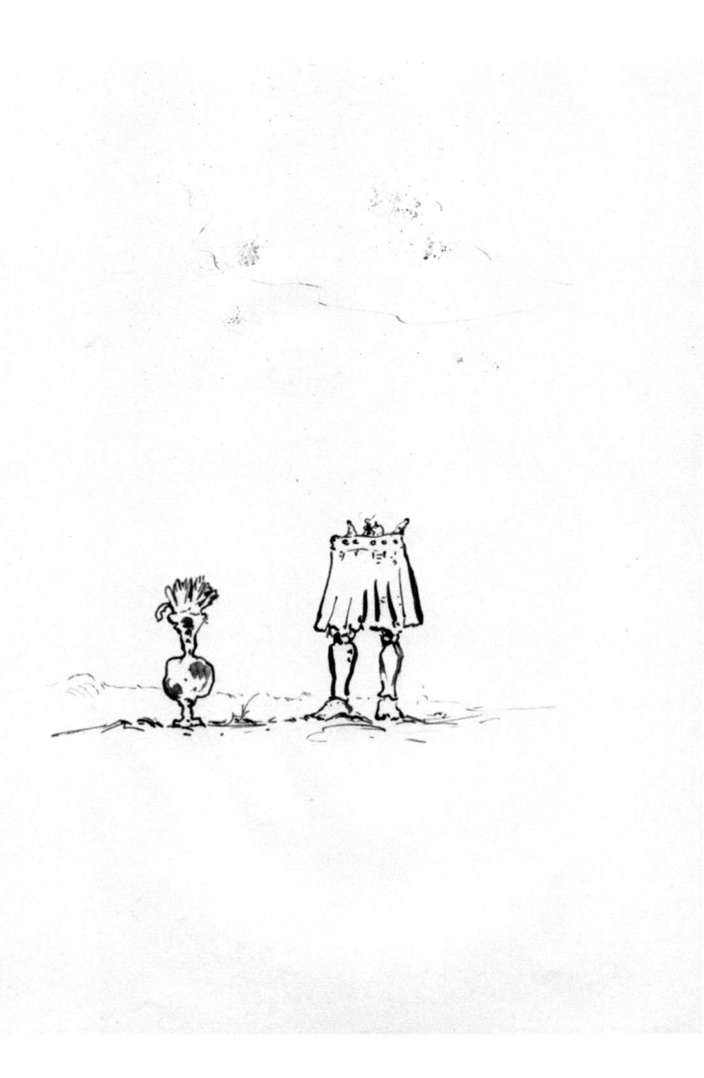

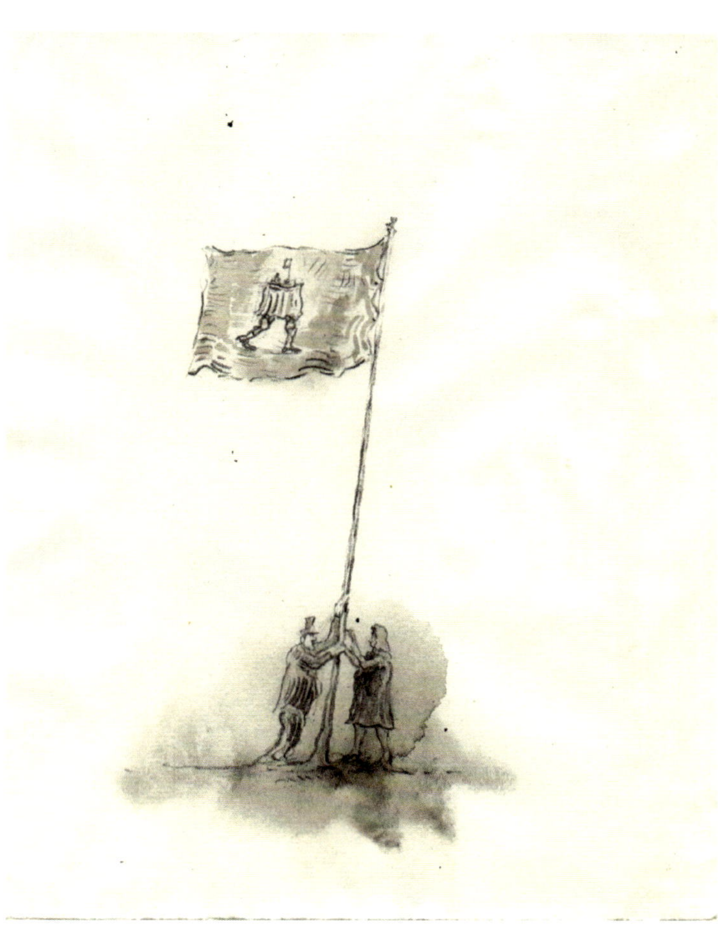

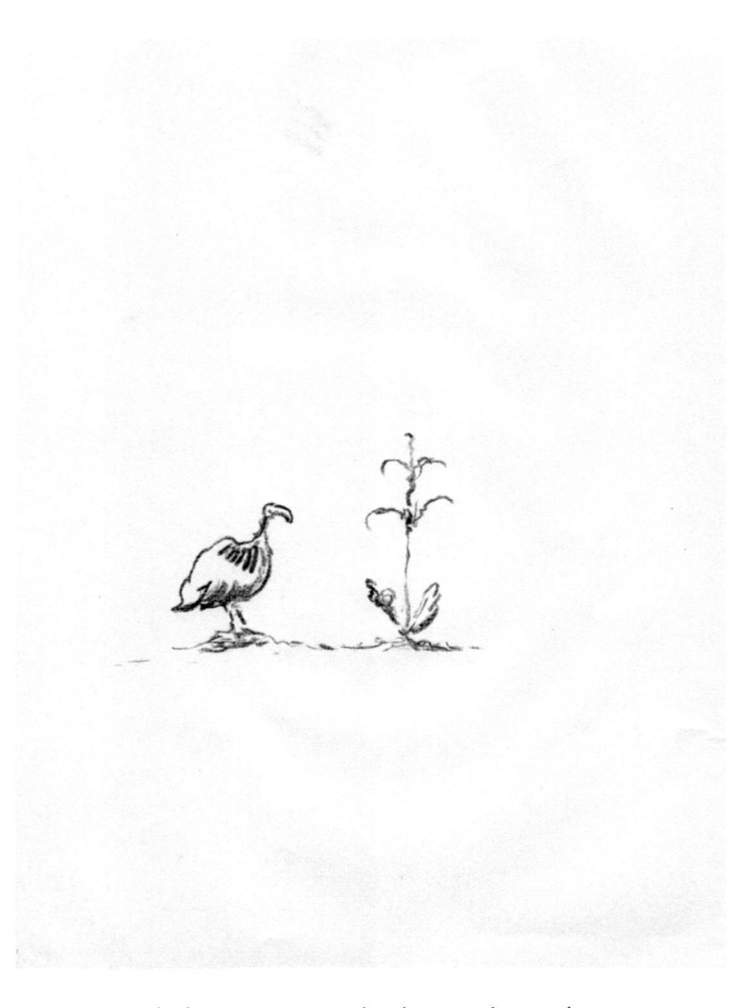

Avis vermem prioris noctis canit.

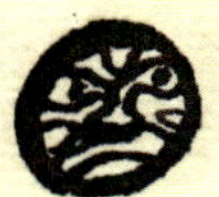

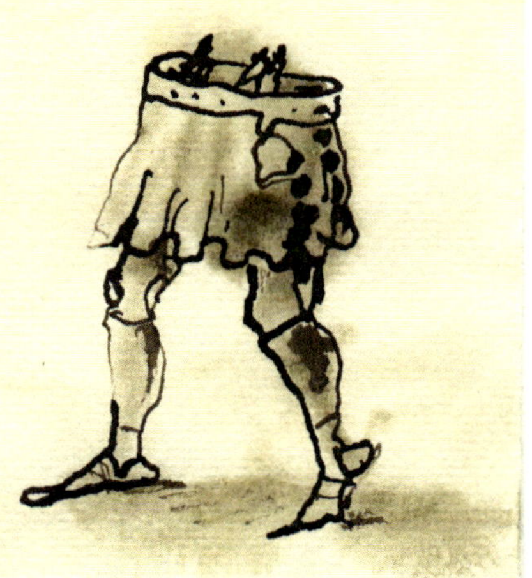

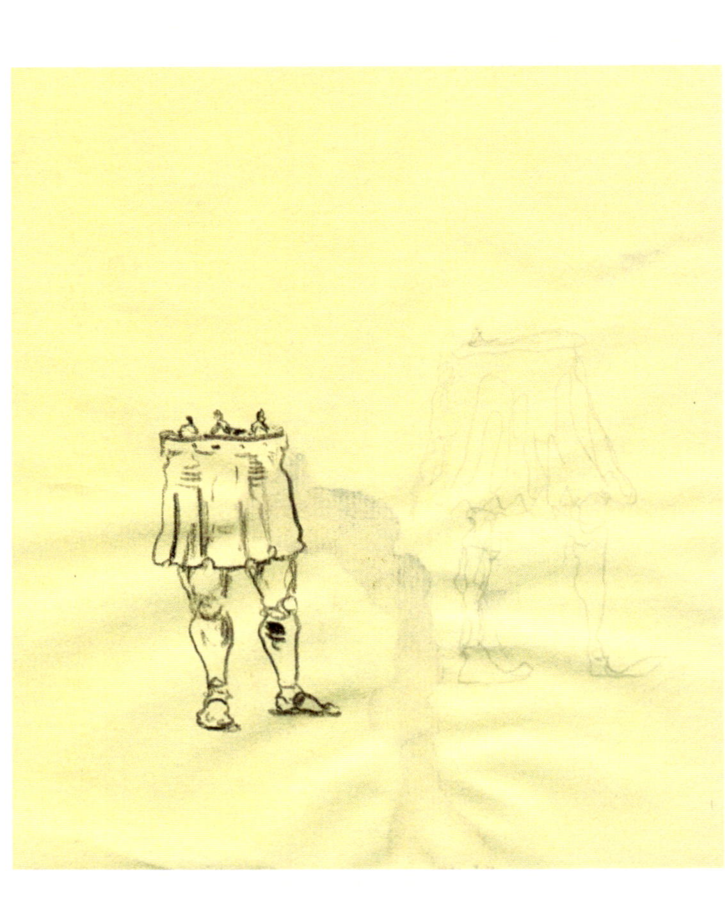

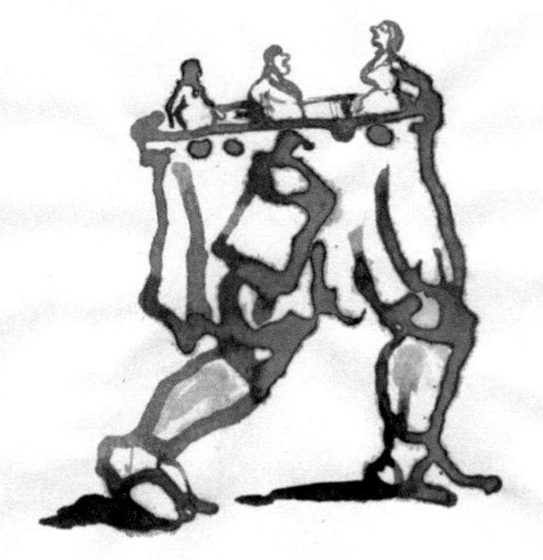

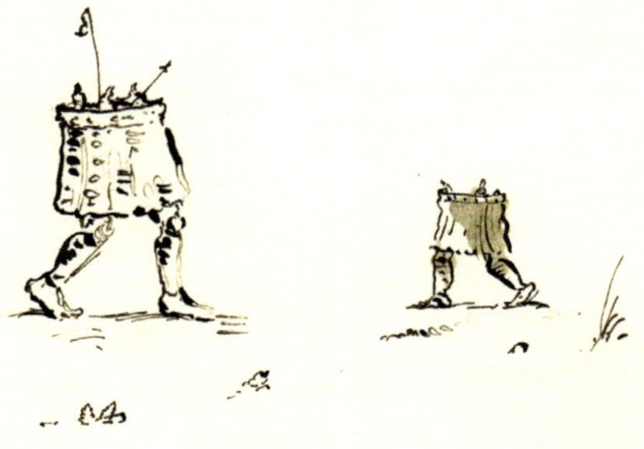

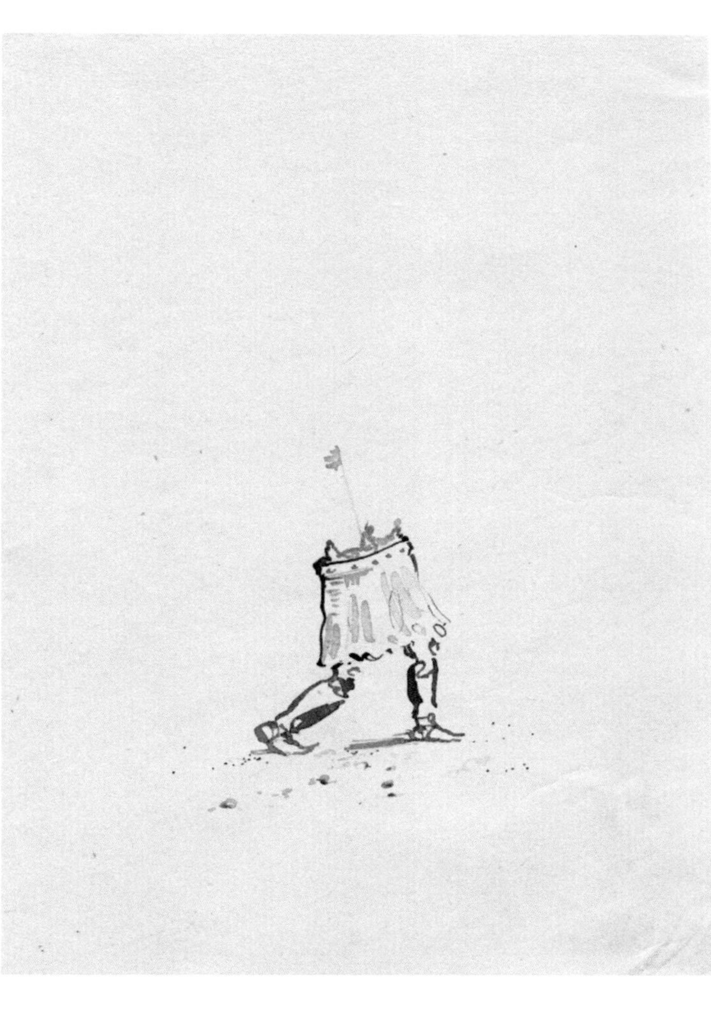

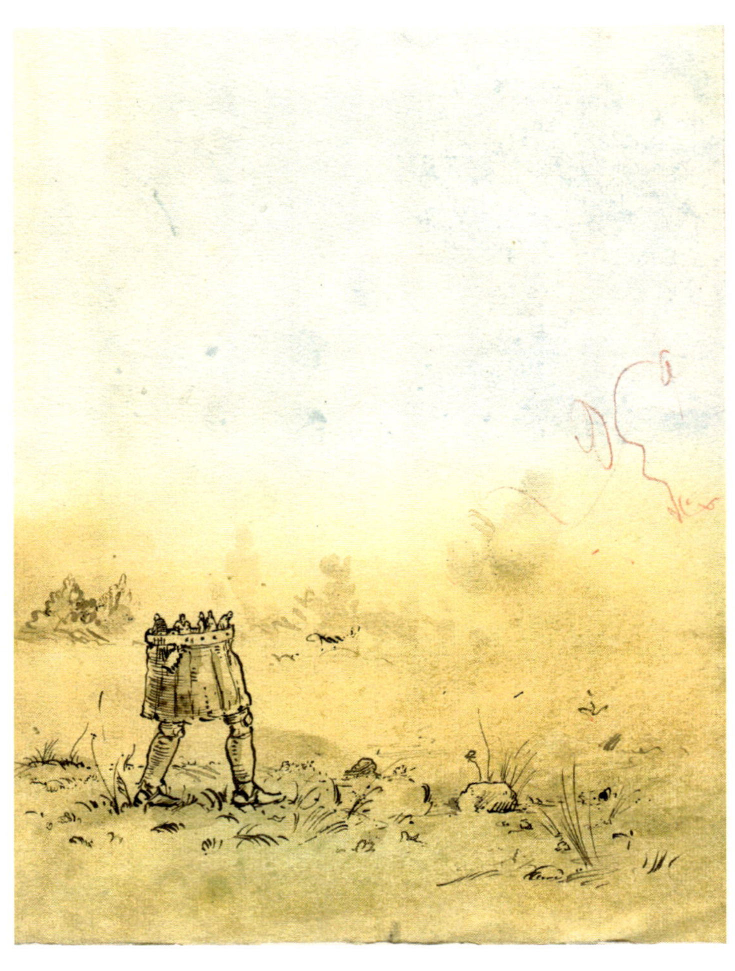

Non sumus plus in camera quam orbe.

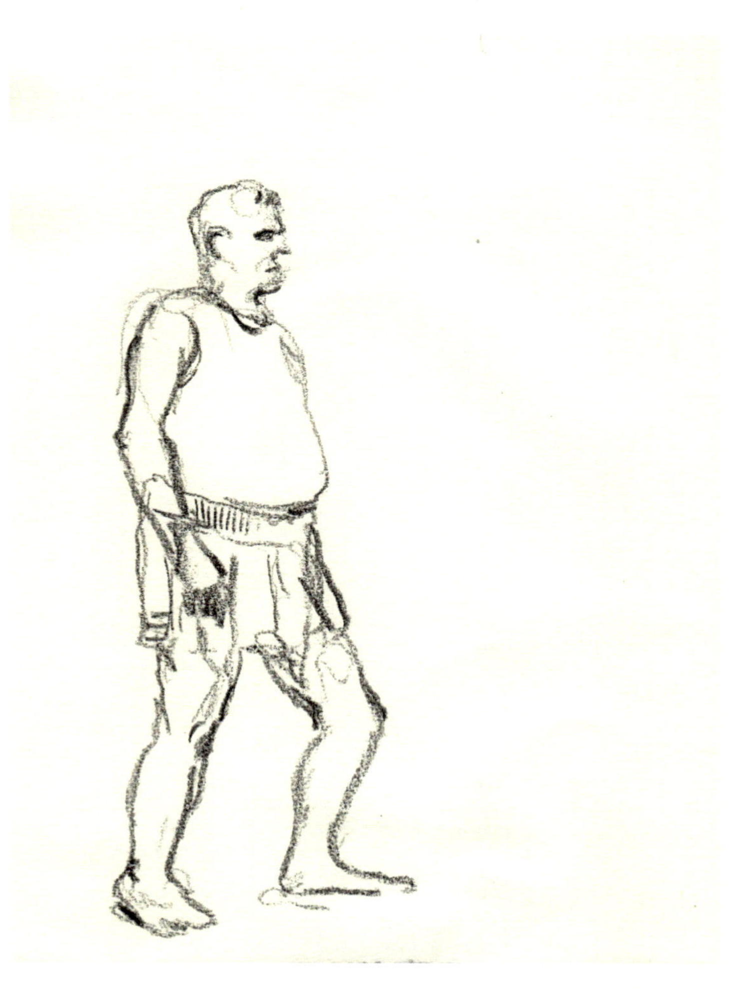

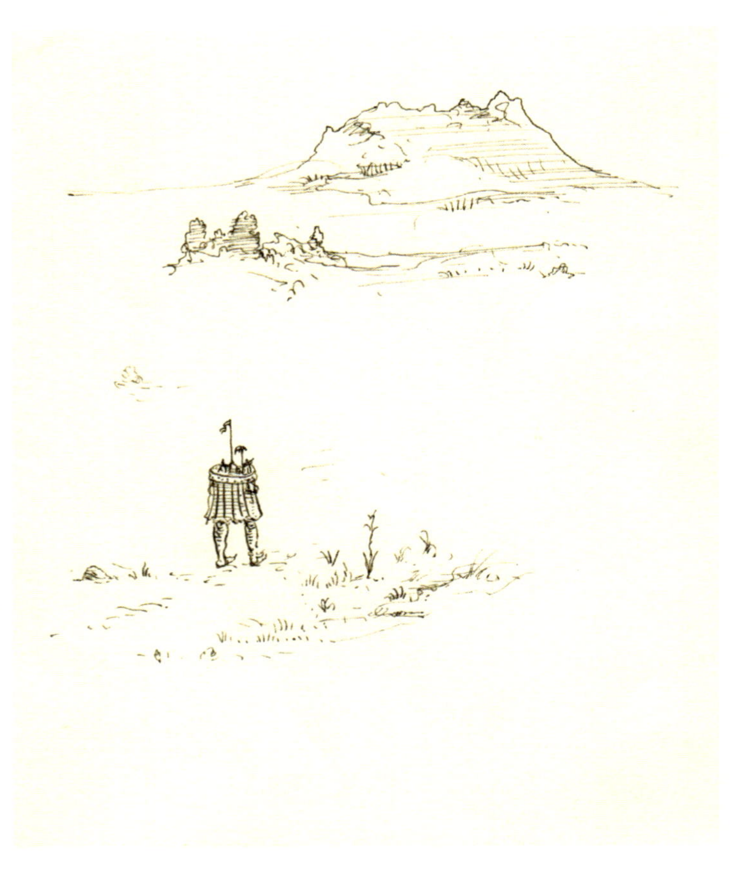

Quo modo oculus rotundus angulum percipit?

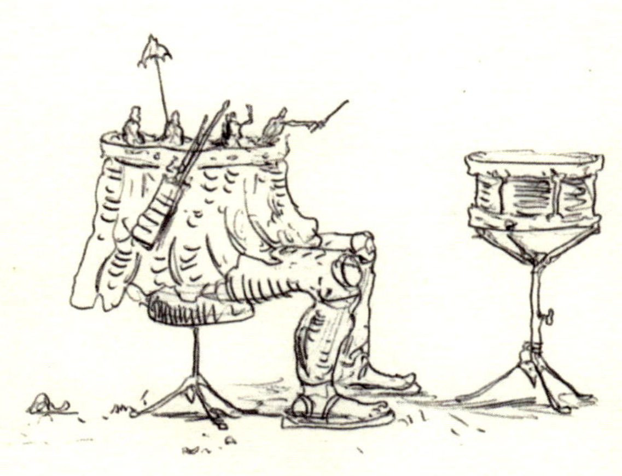

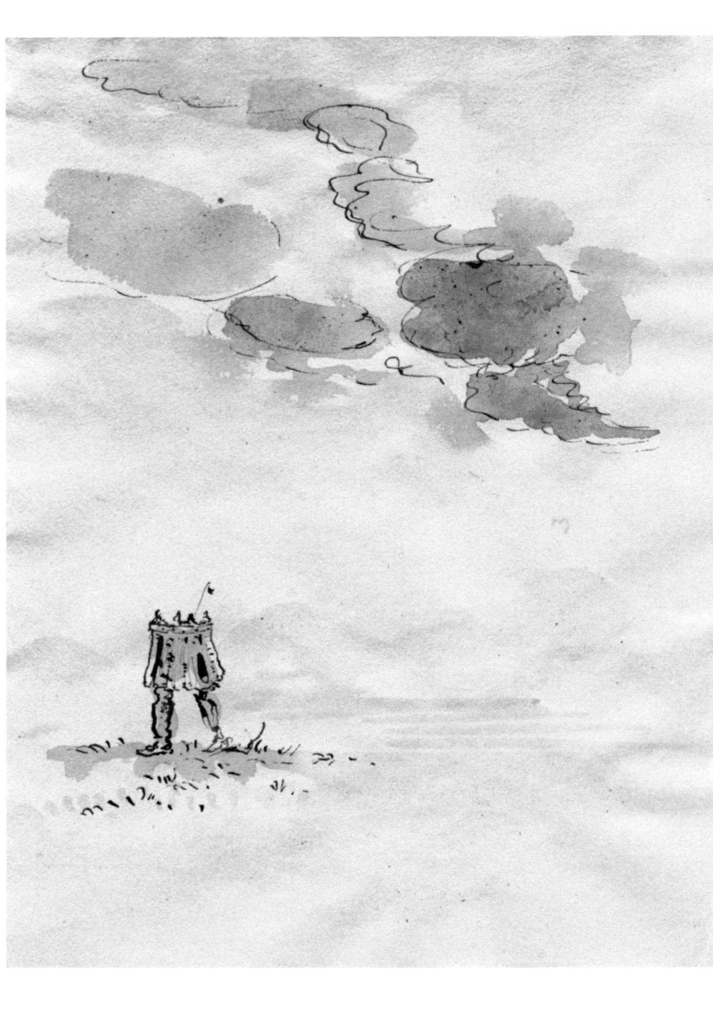

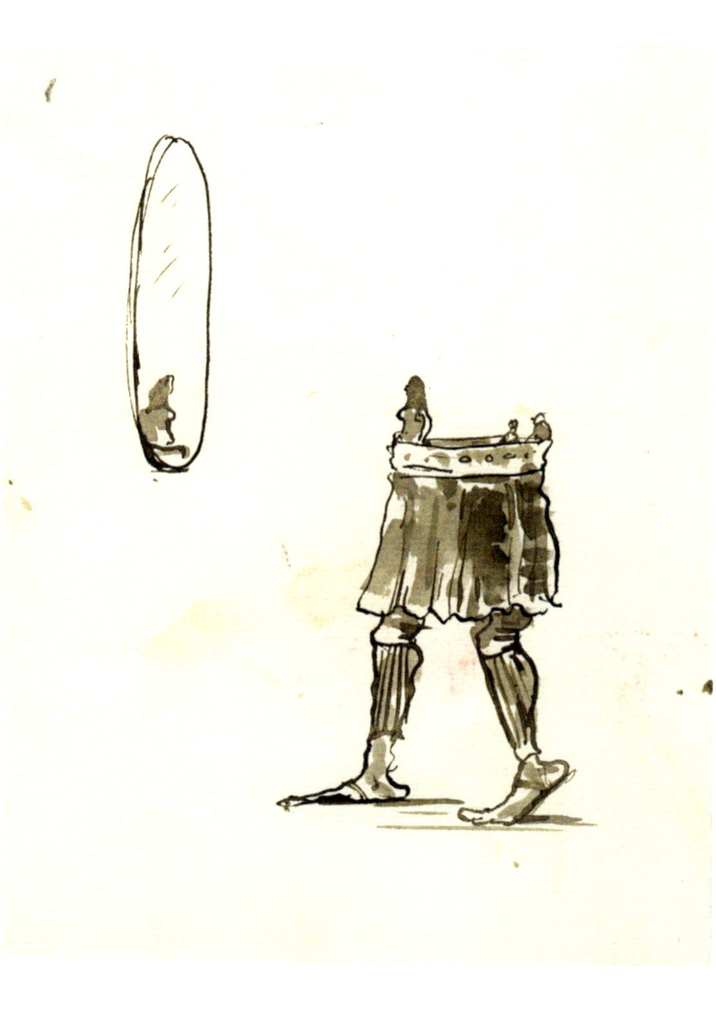

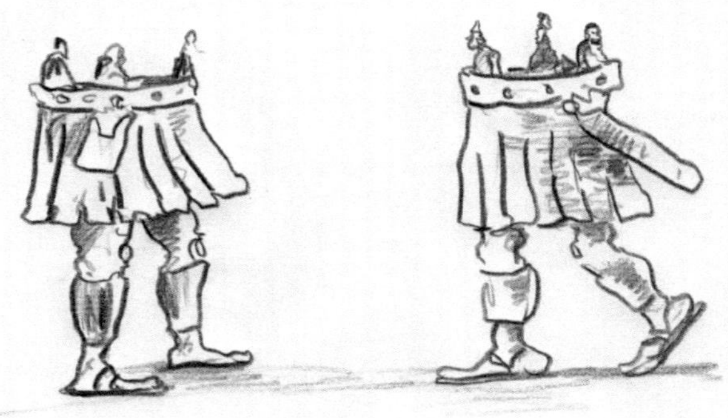
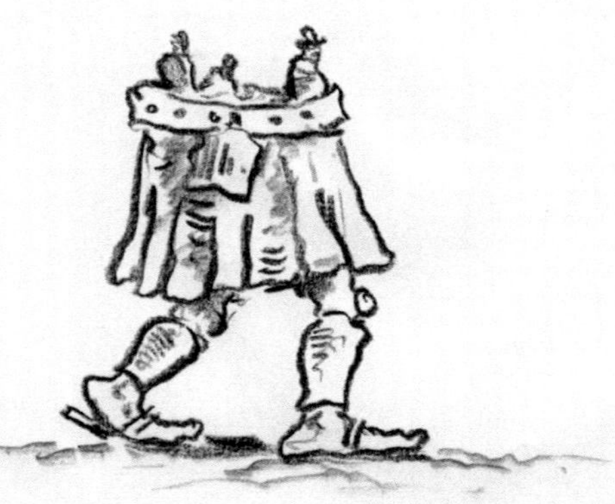

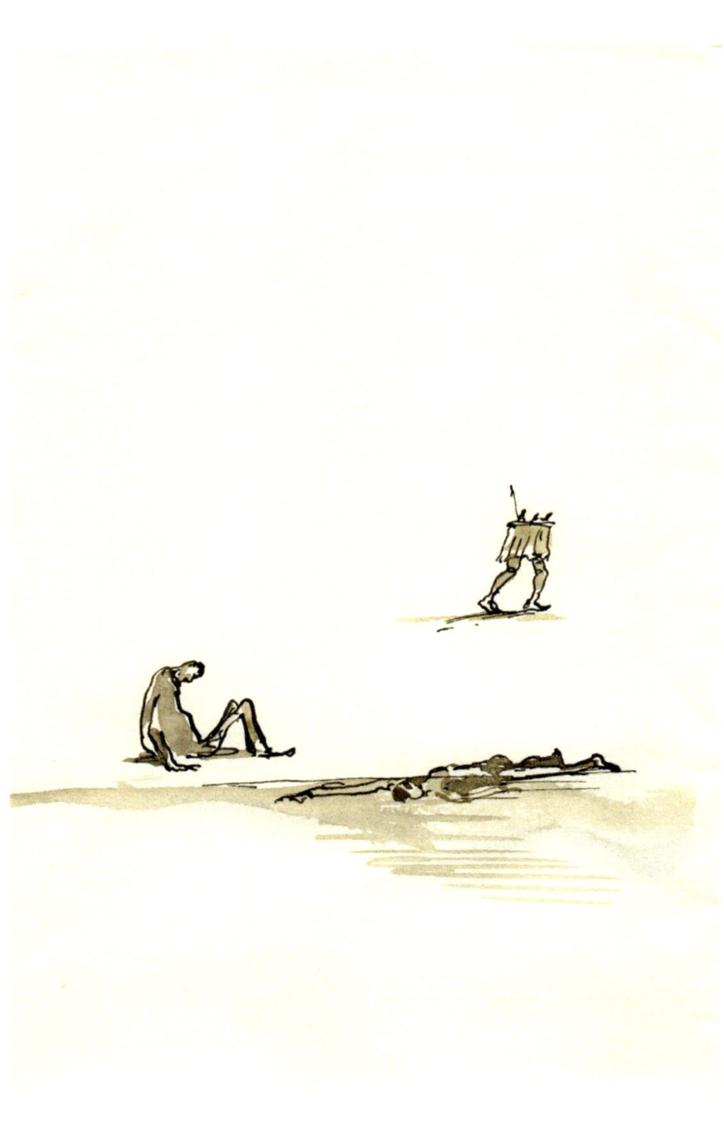

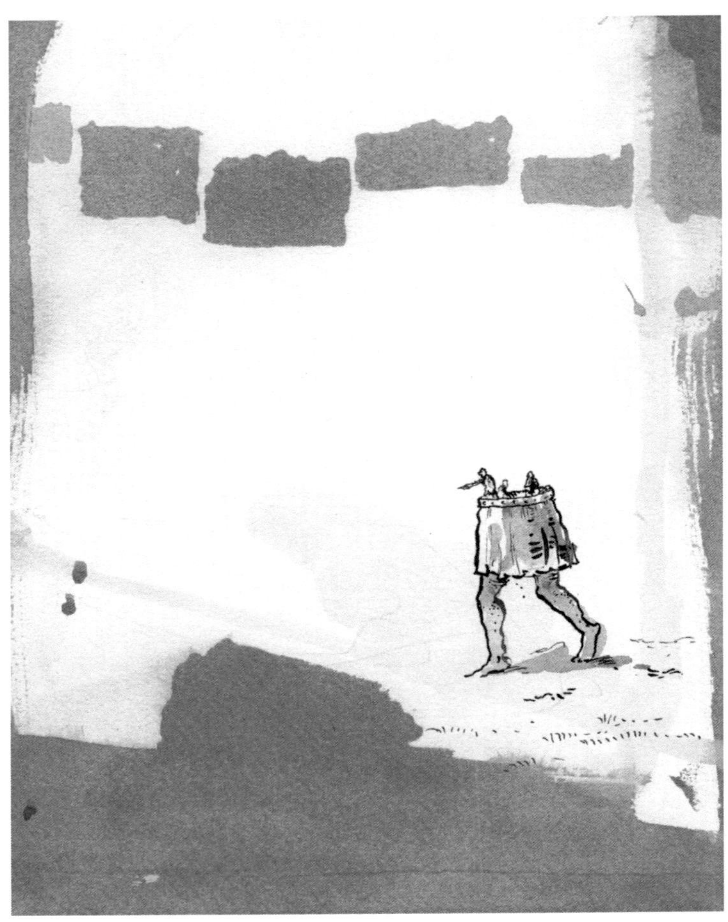

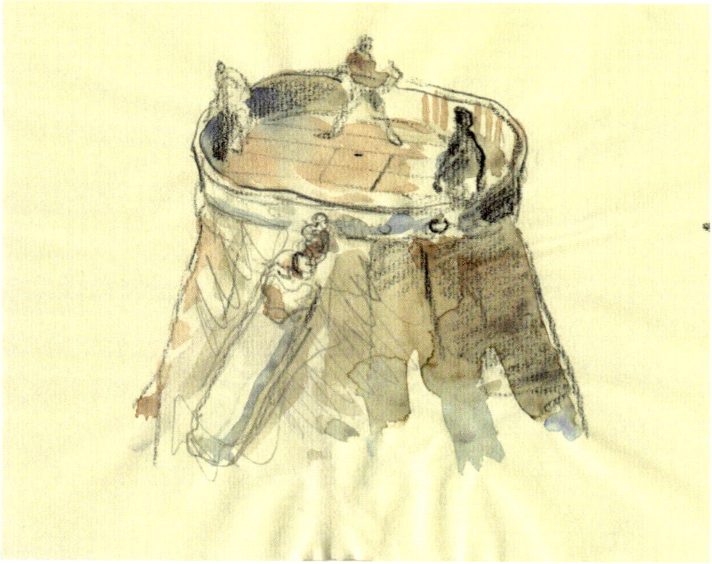

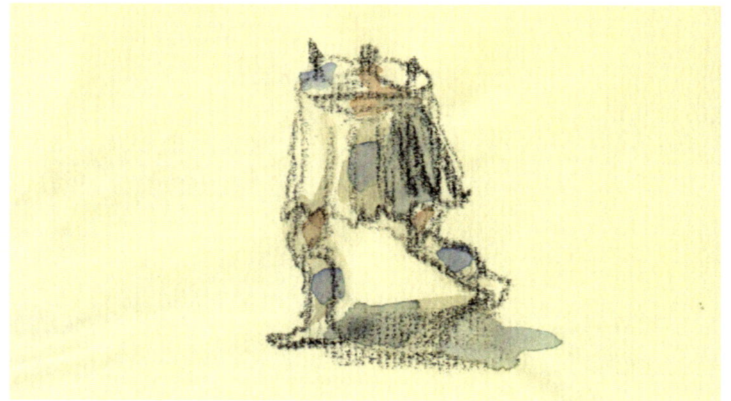

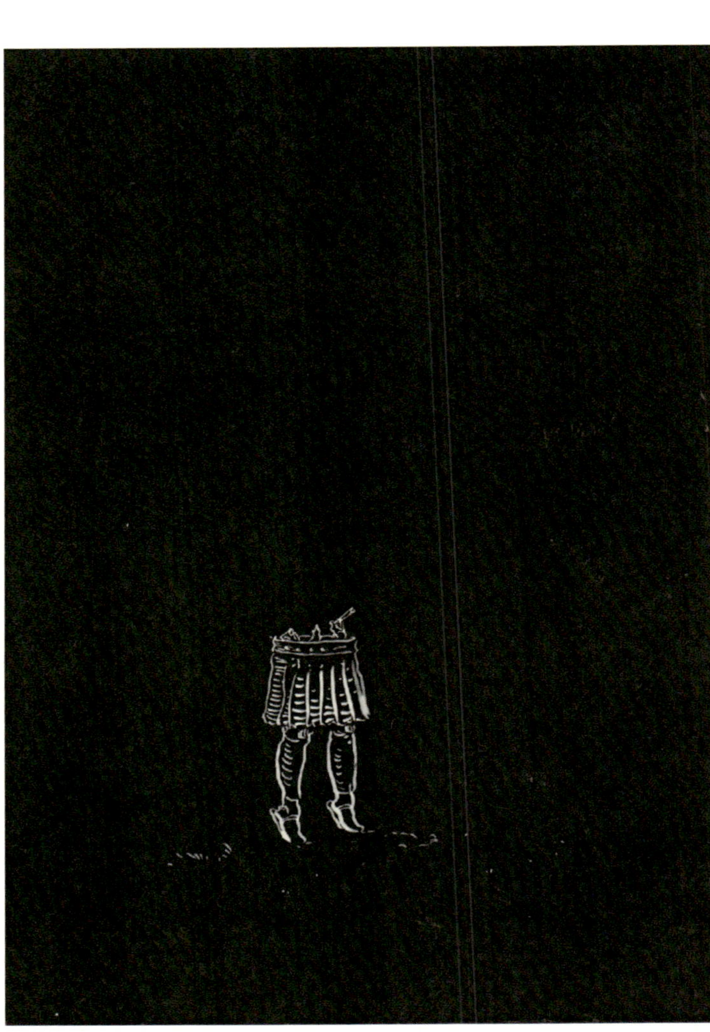

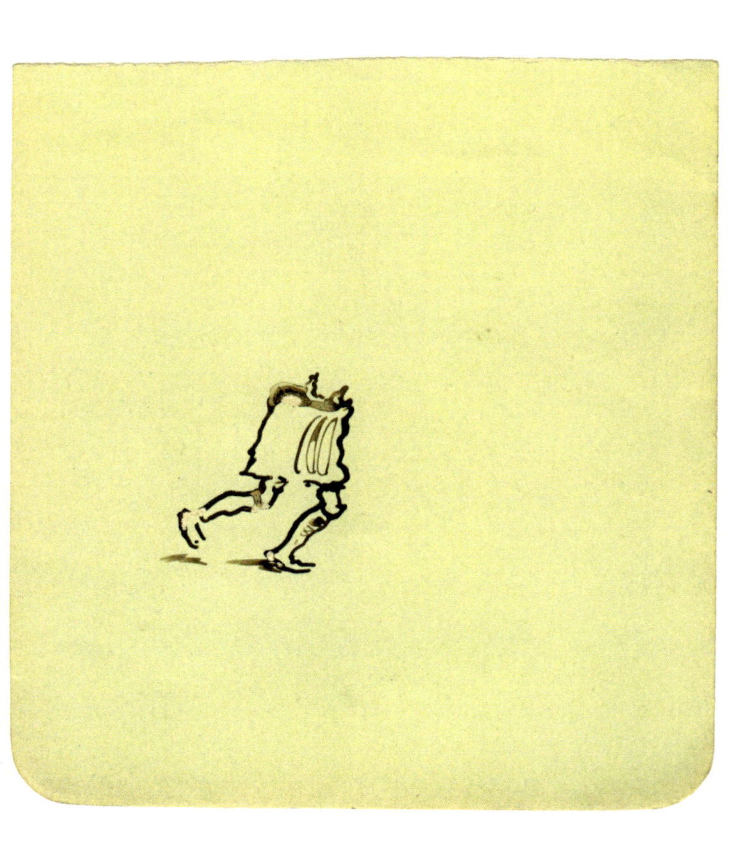

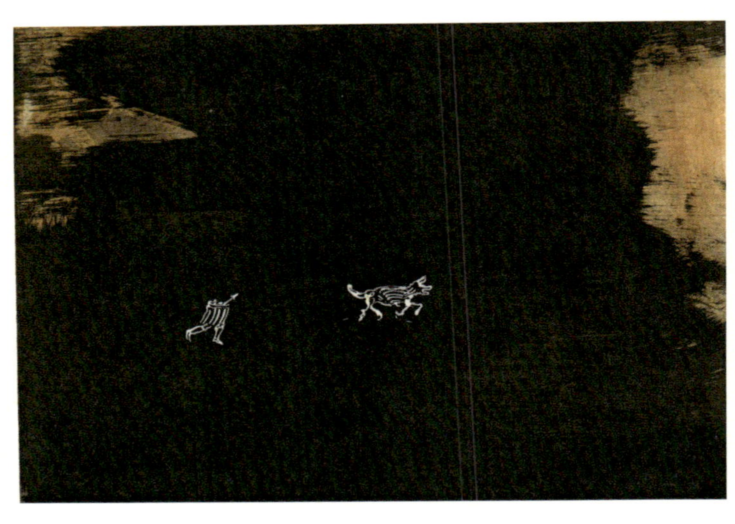

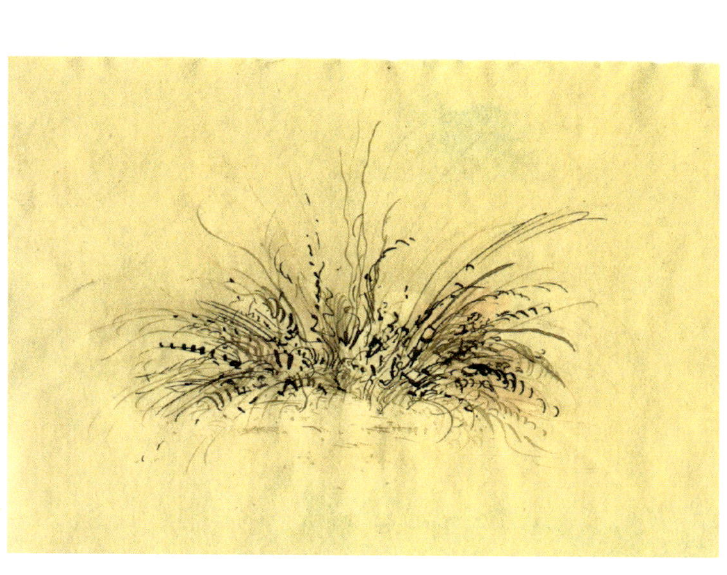

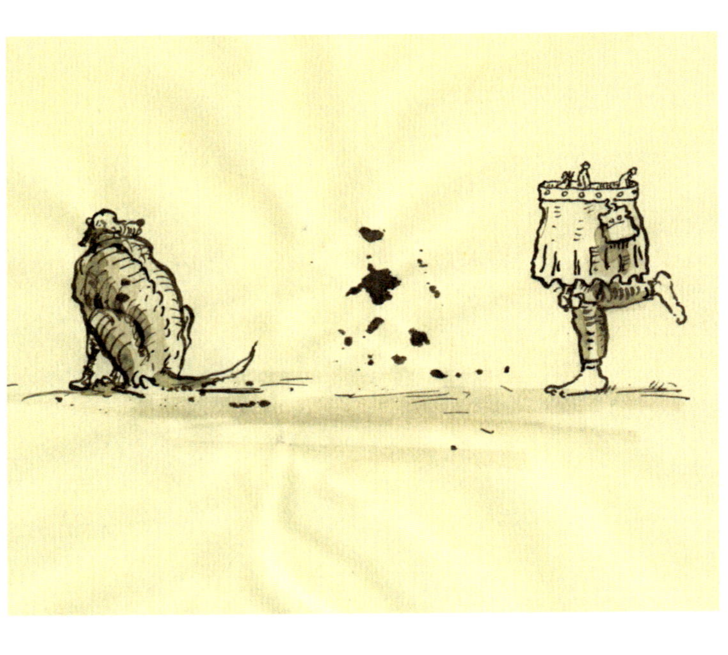

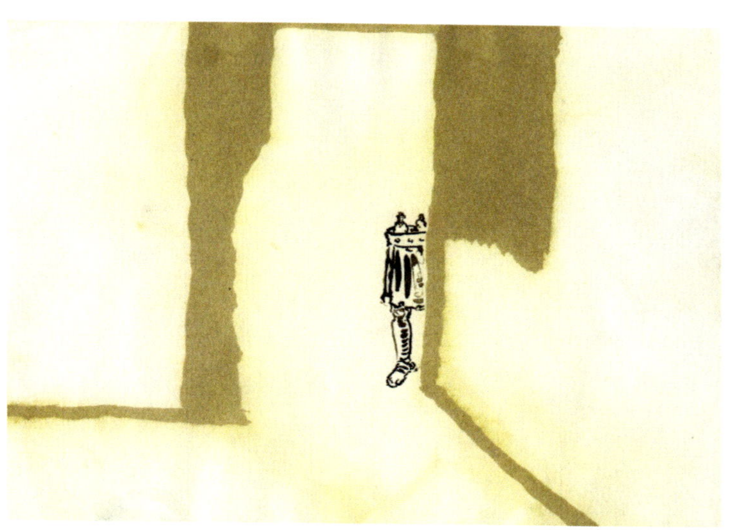

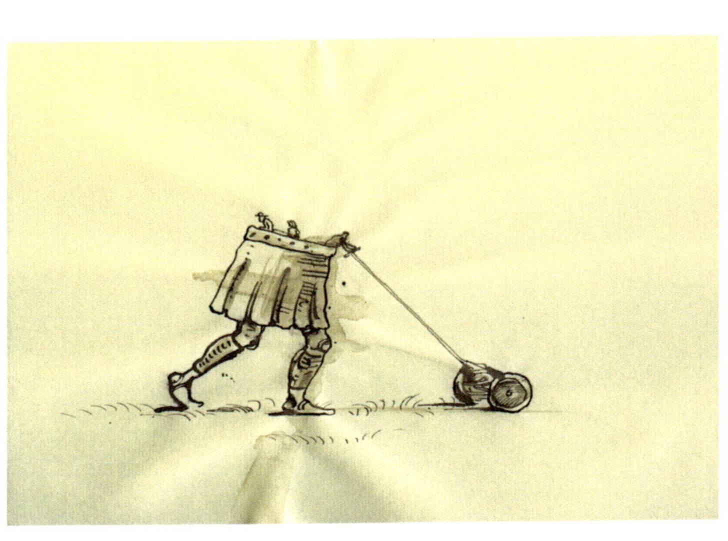

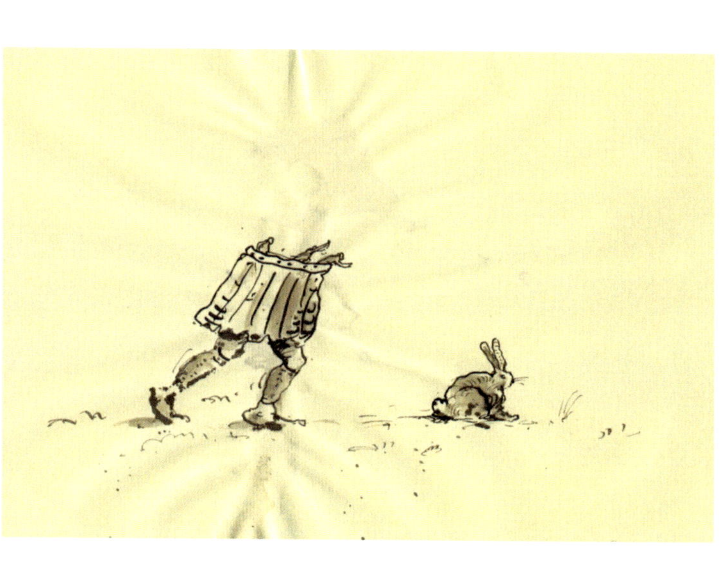

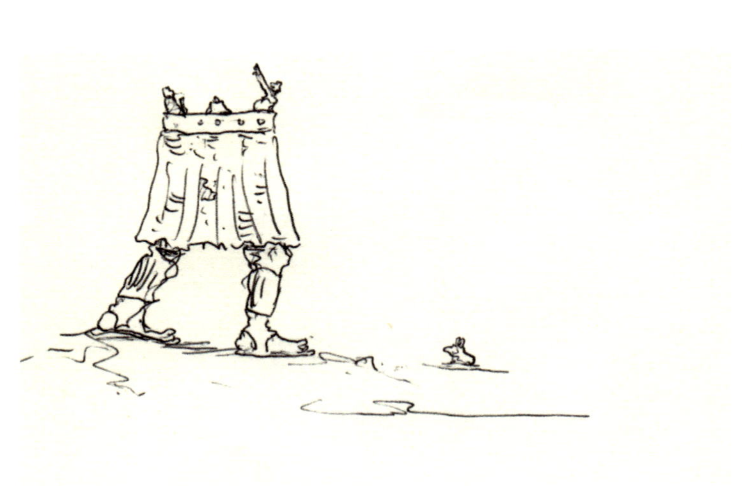

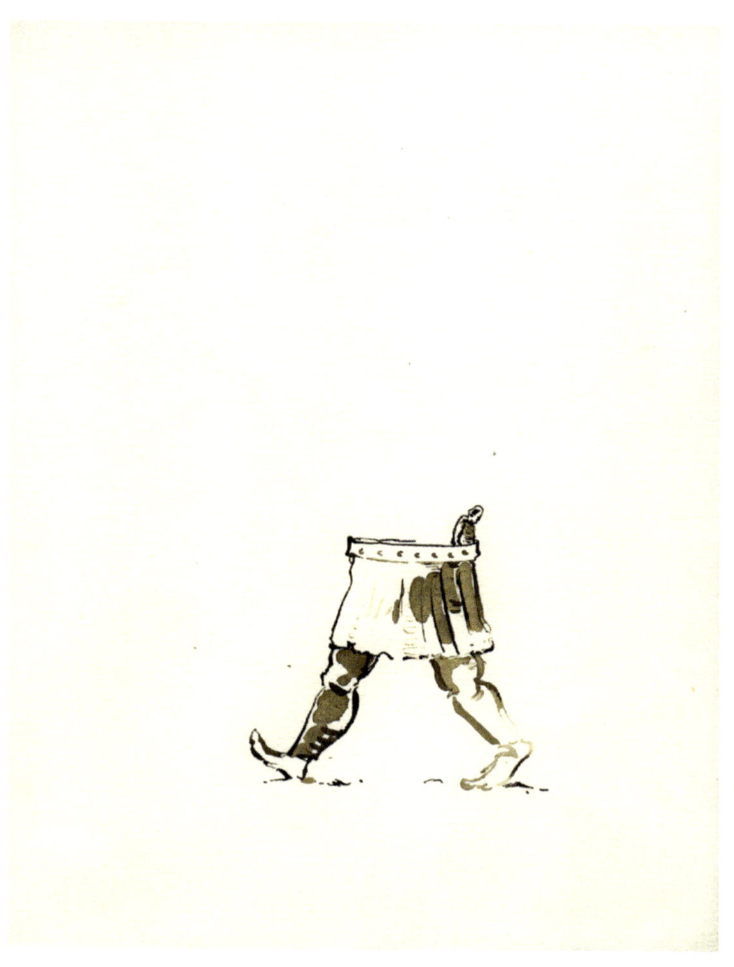

Magna saxa Iovis.

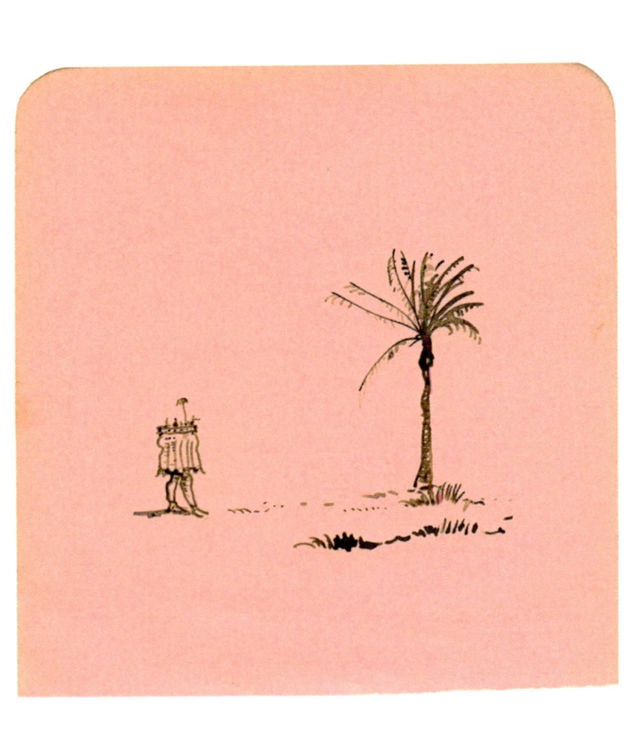

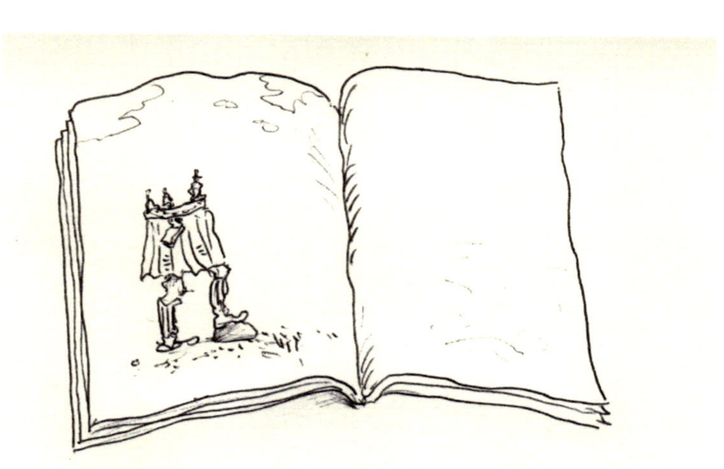

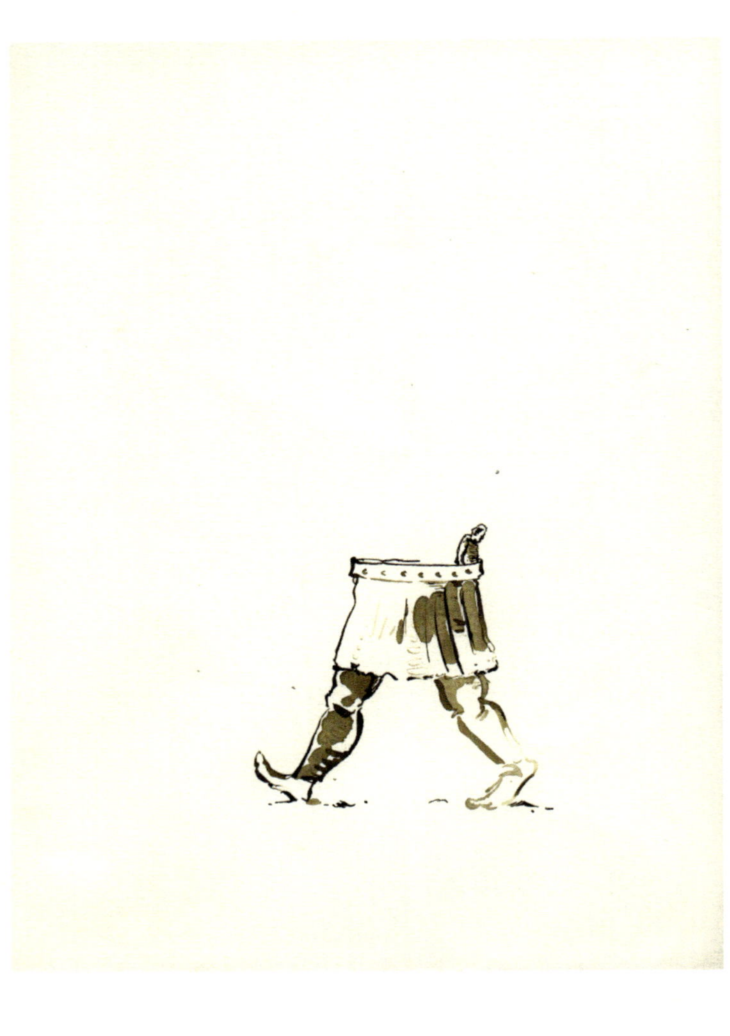

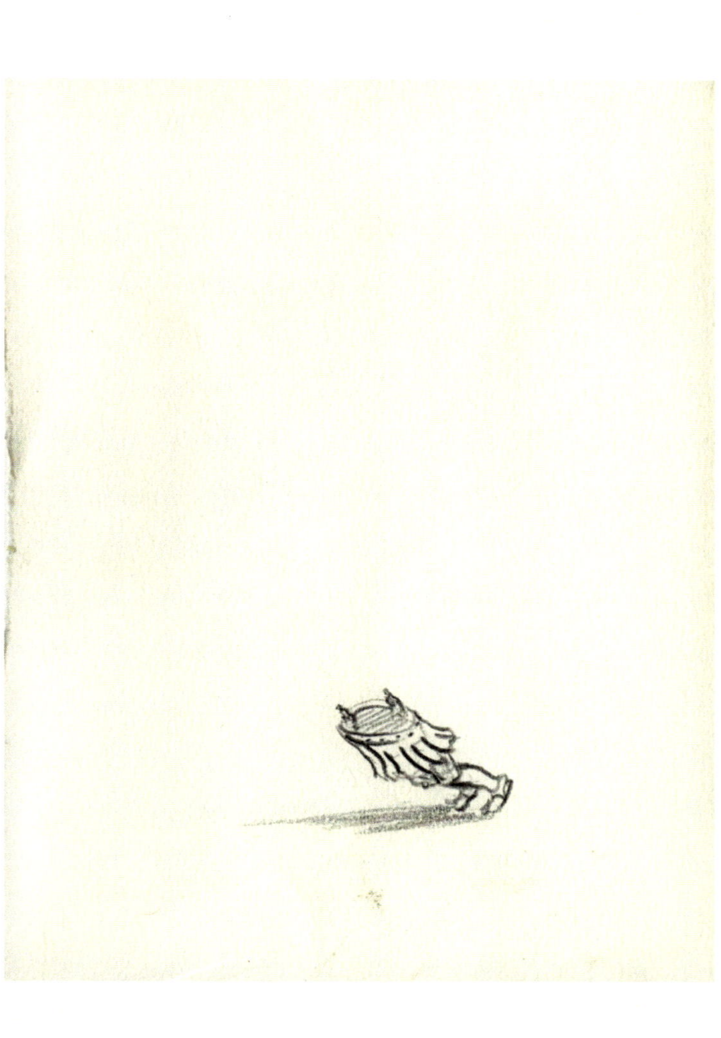

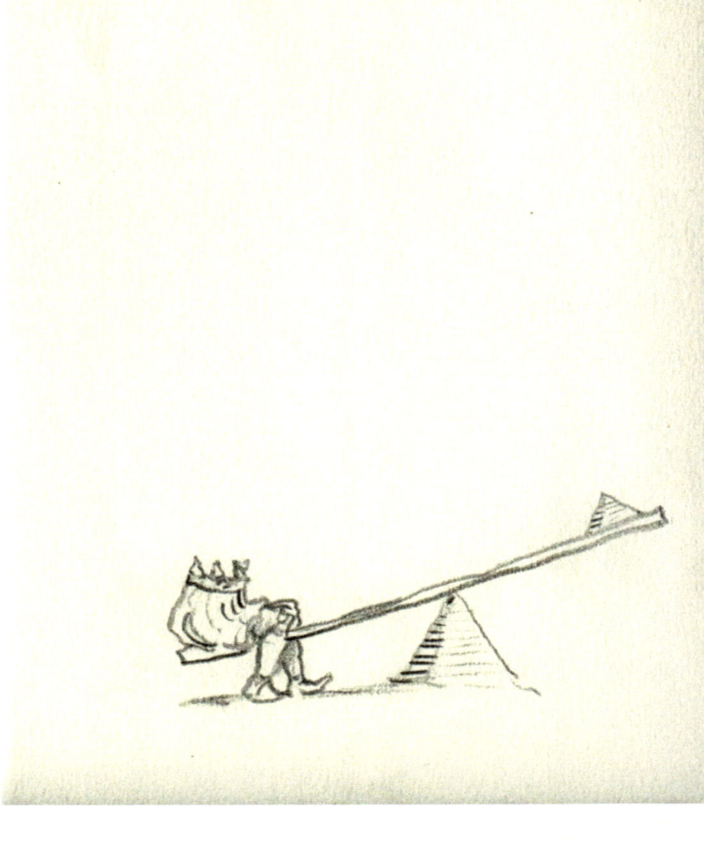

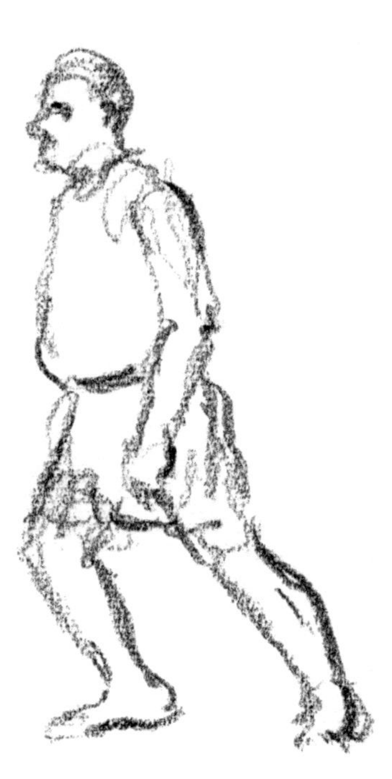

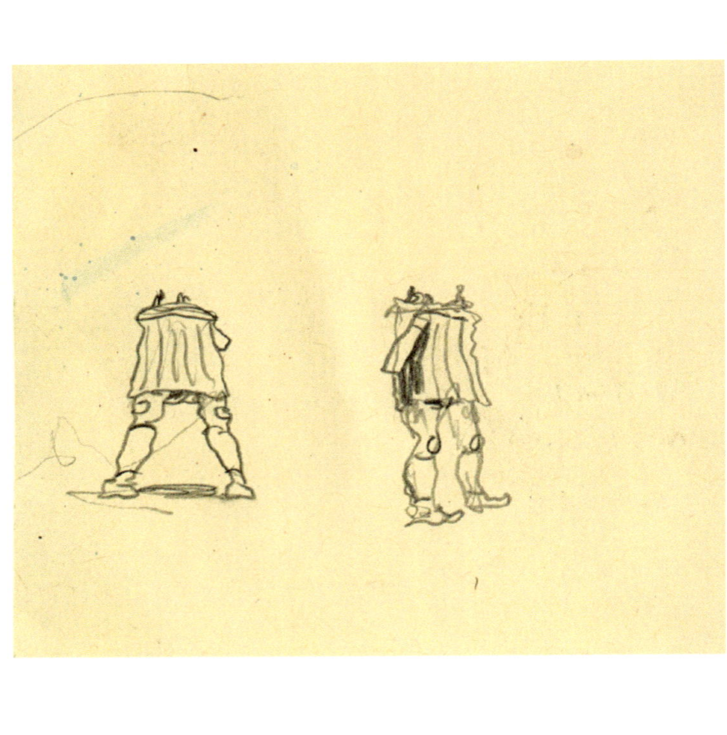

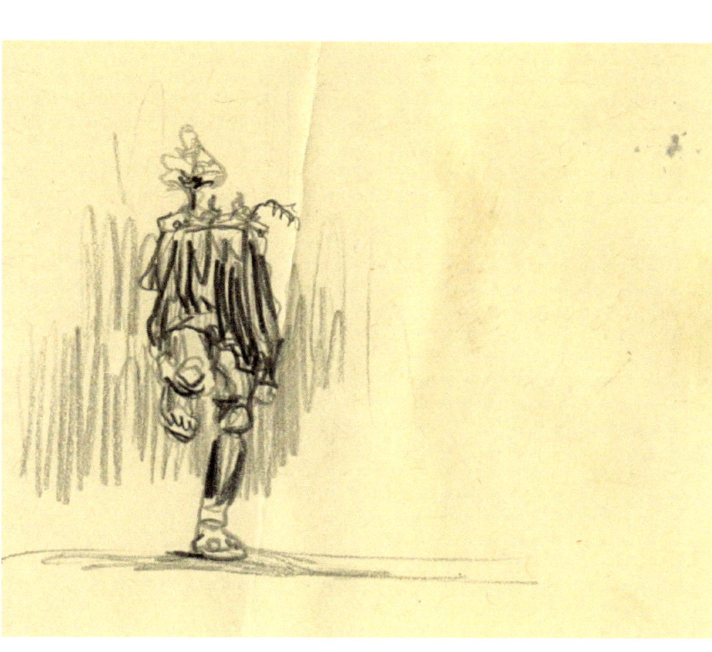

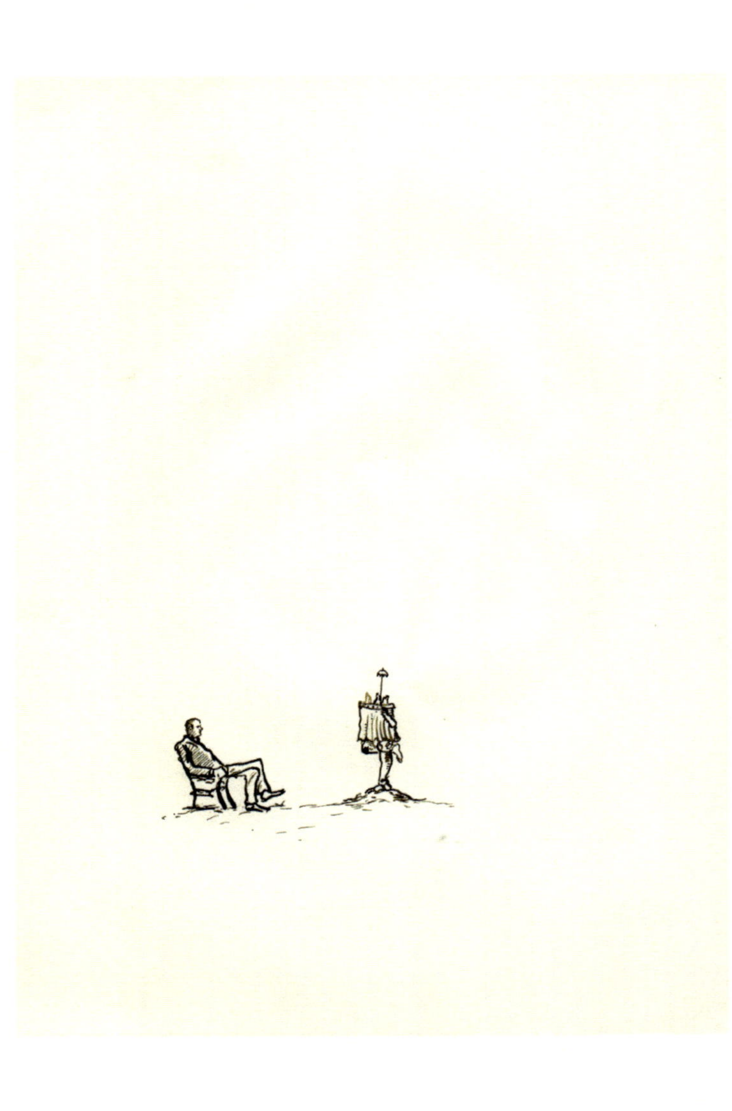

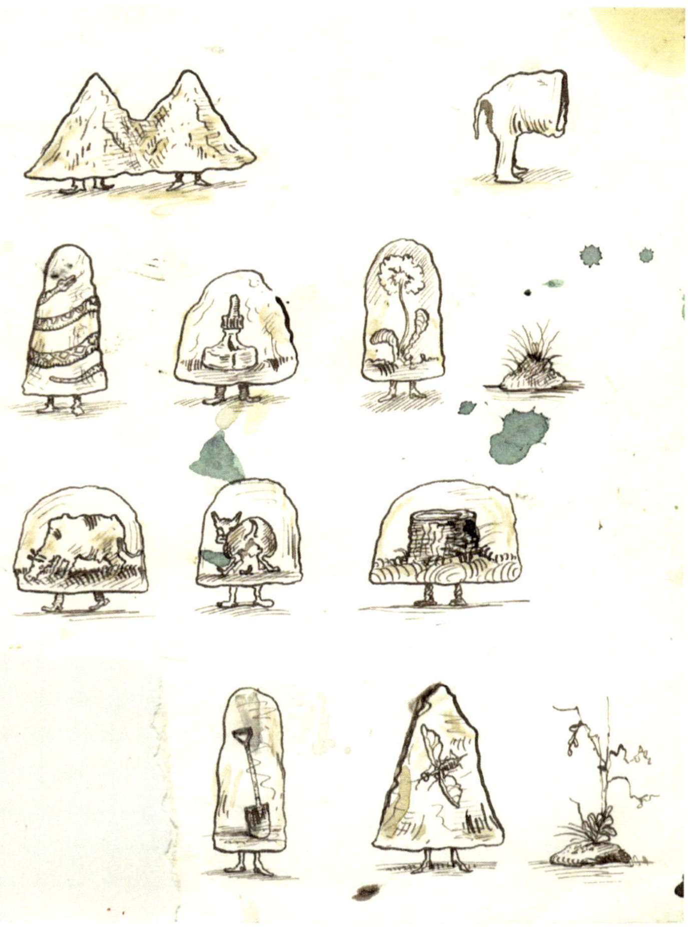

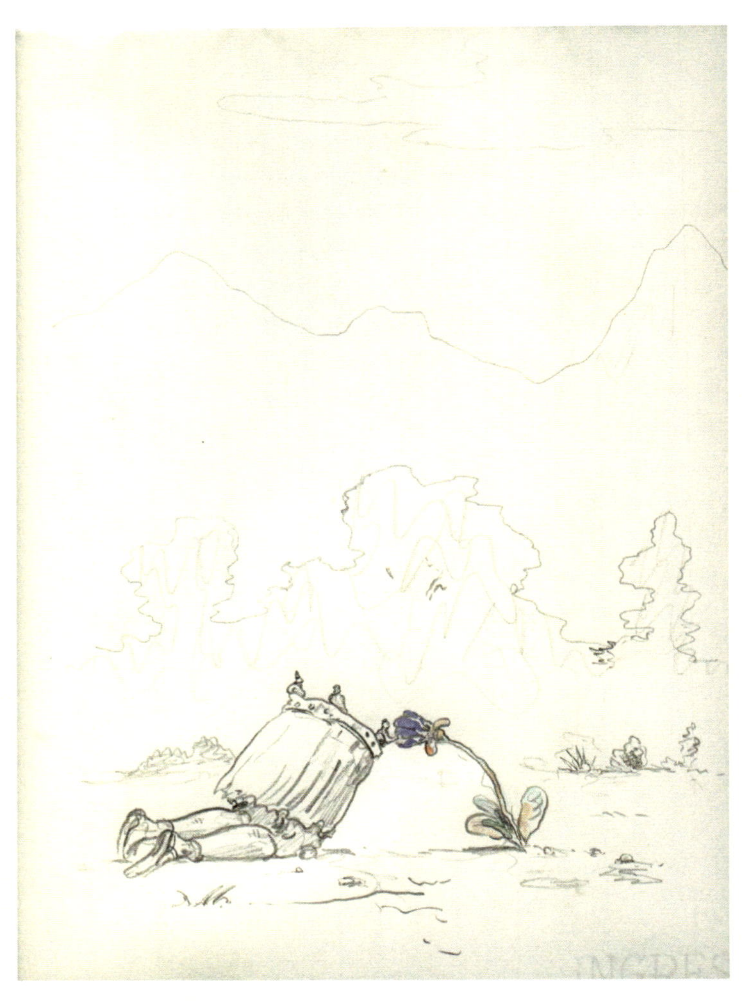

Ecce flores. Olfactum eamus!

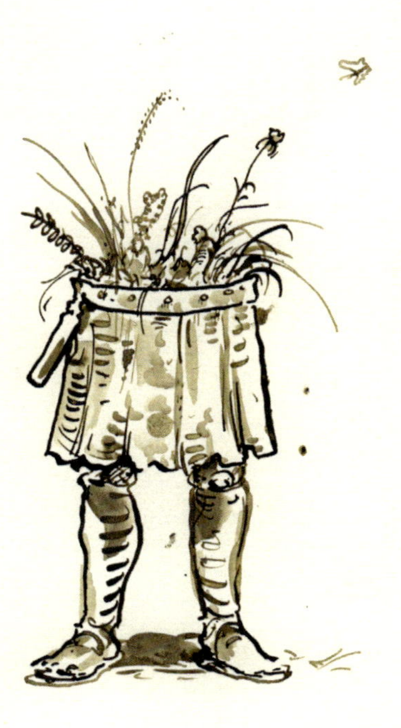

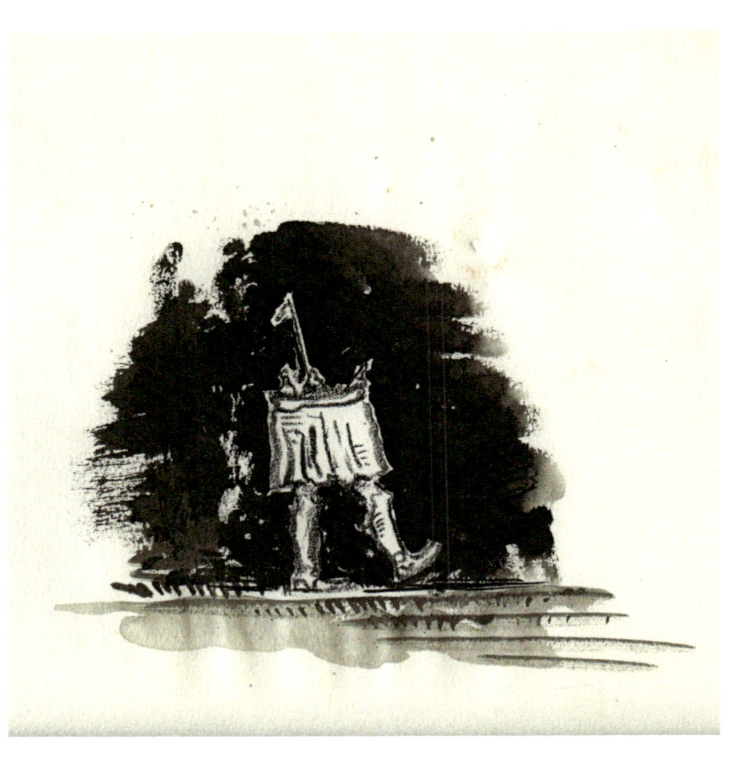

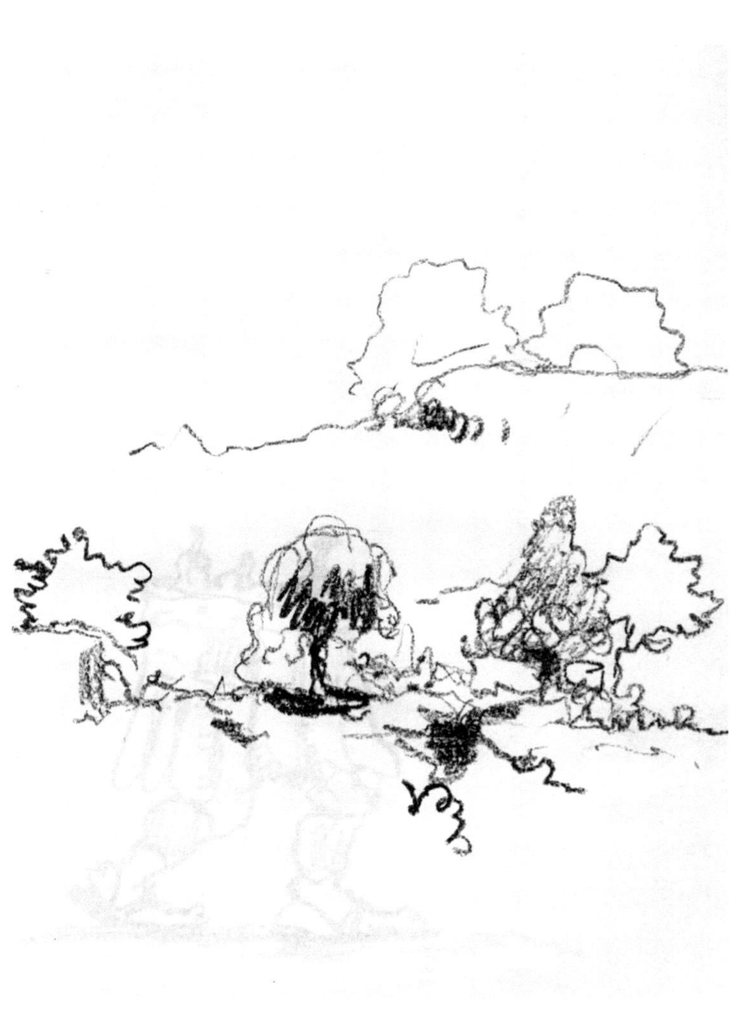

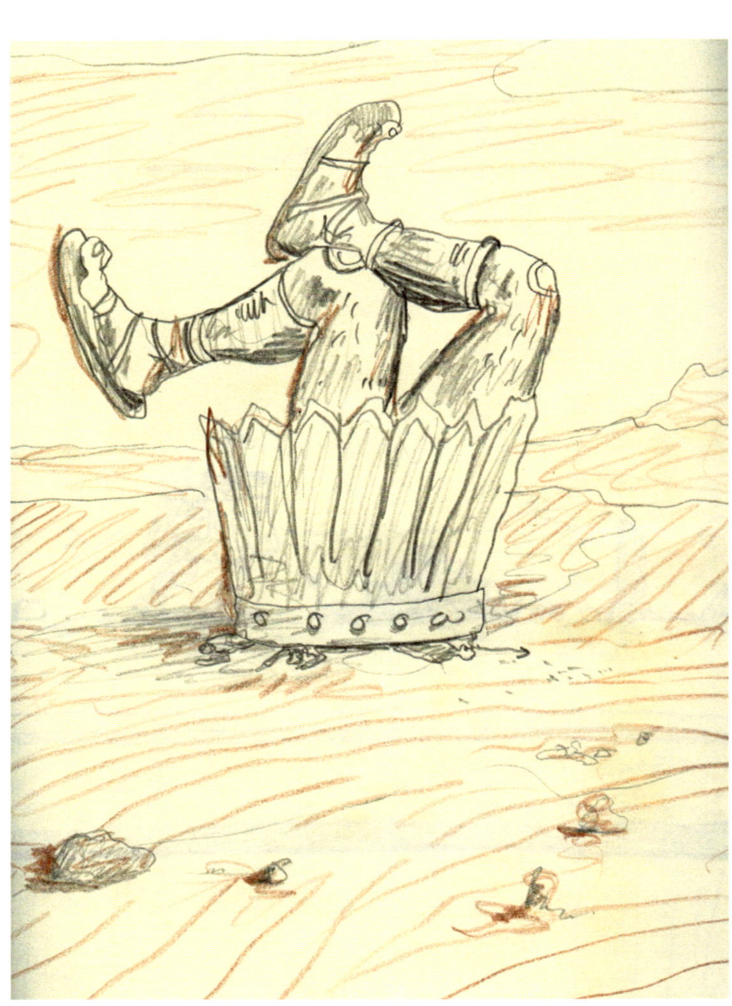

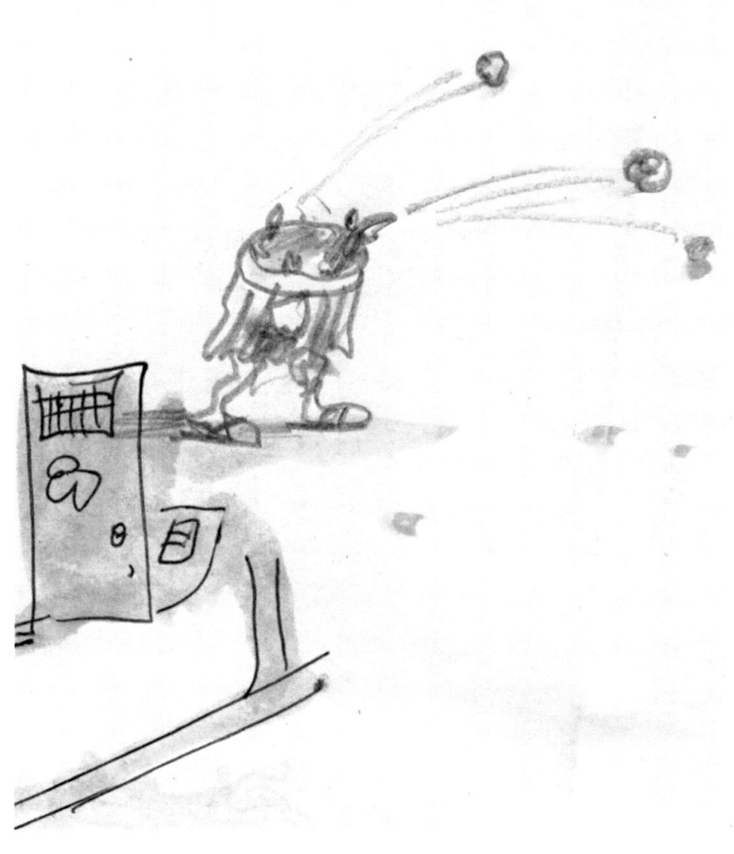

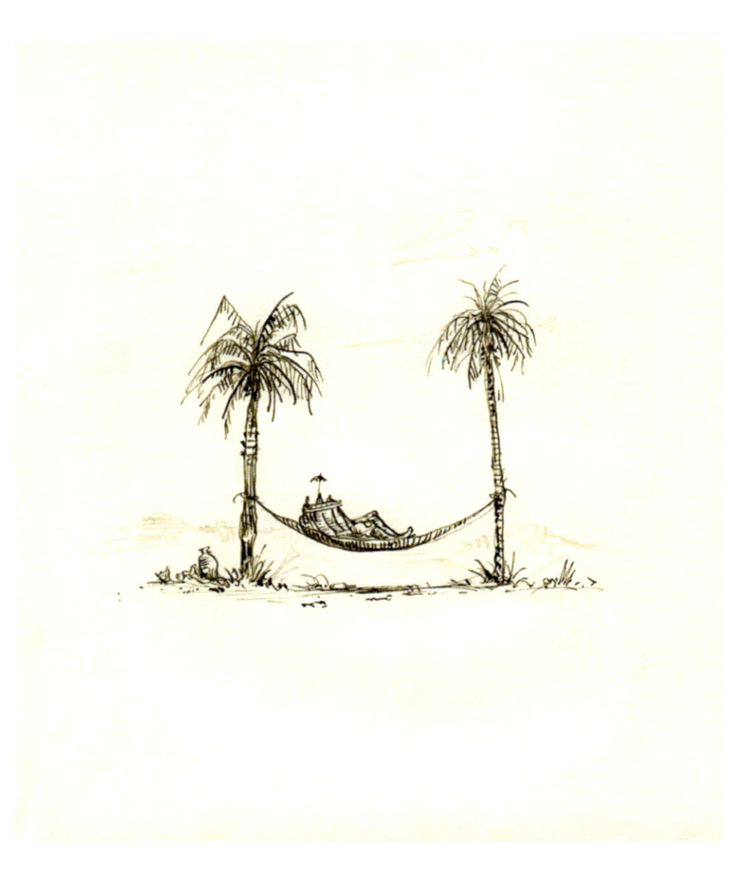

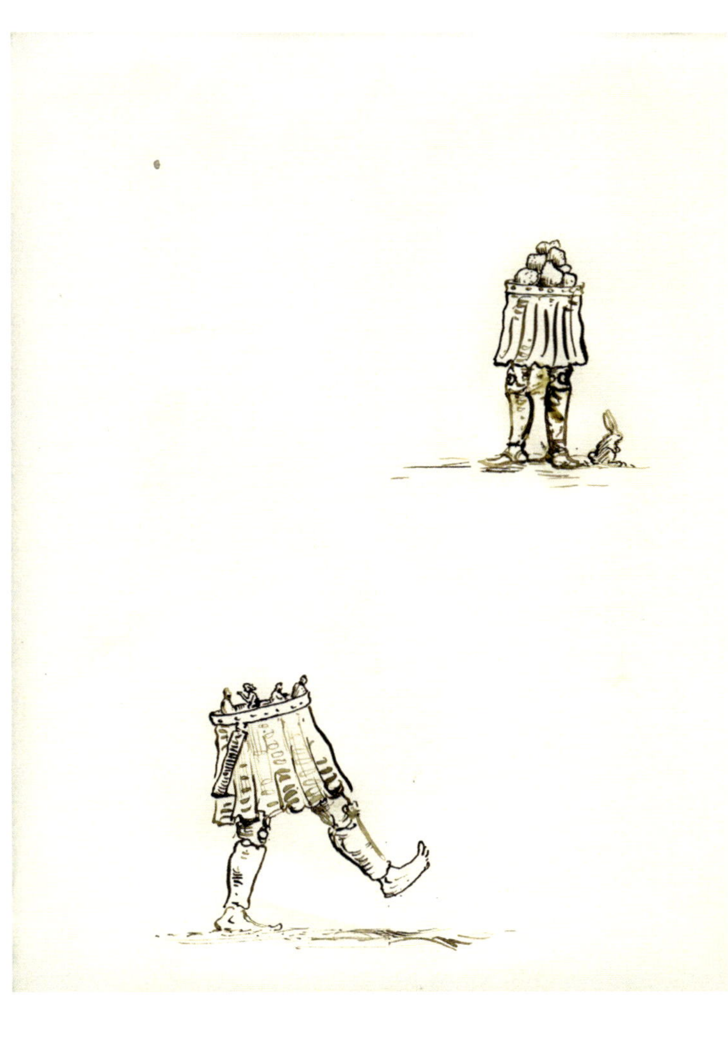

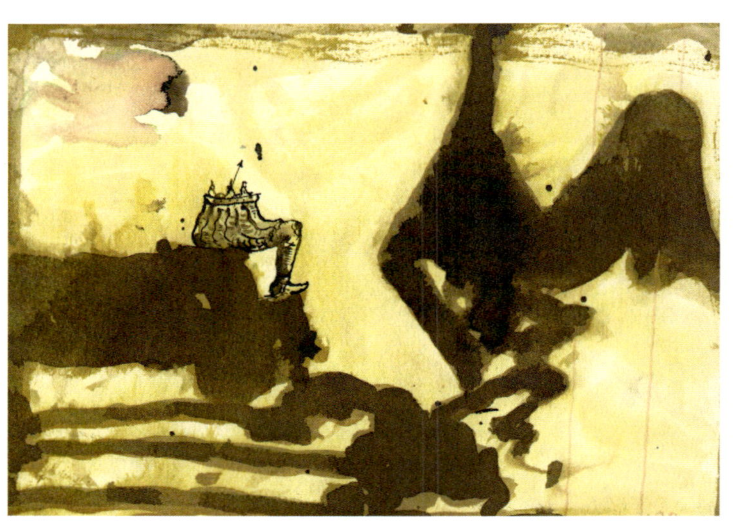

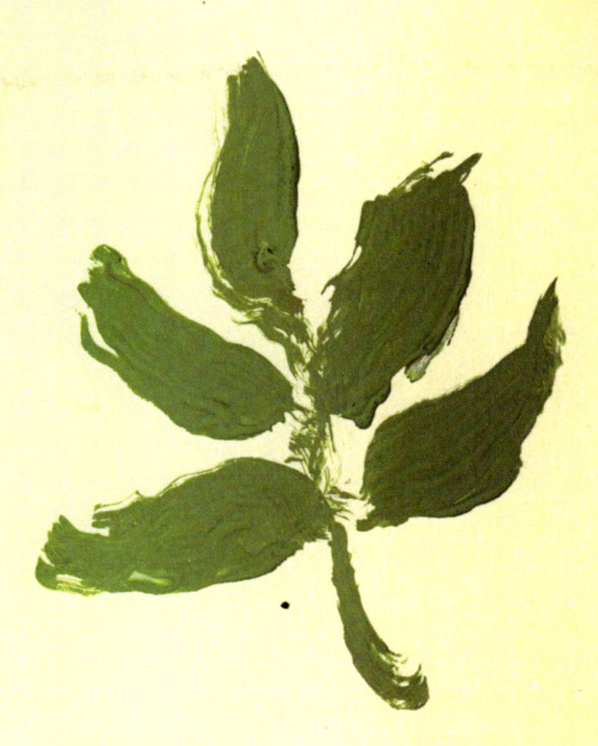

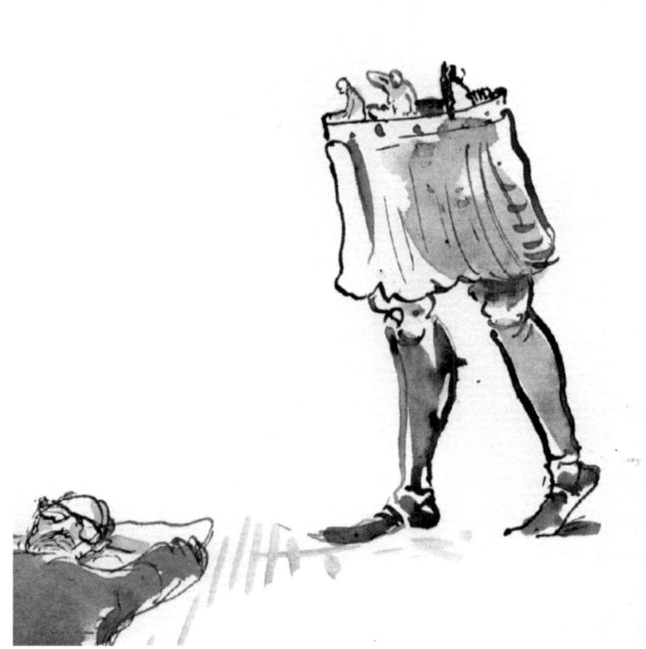

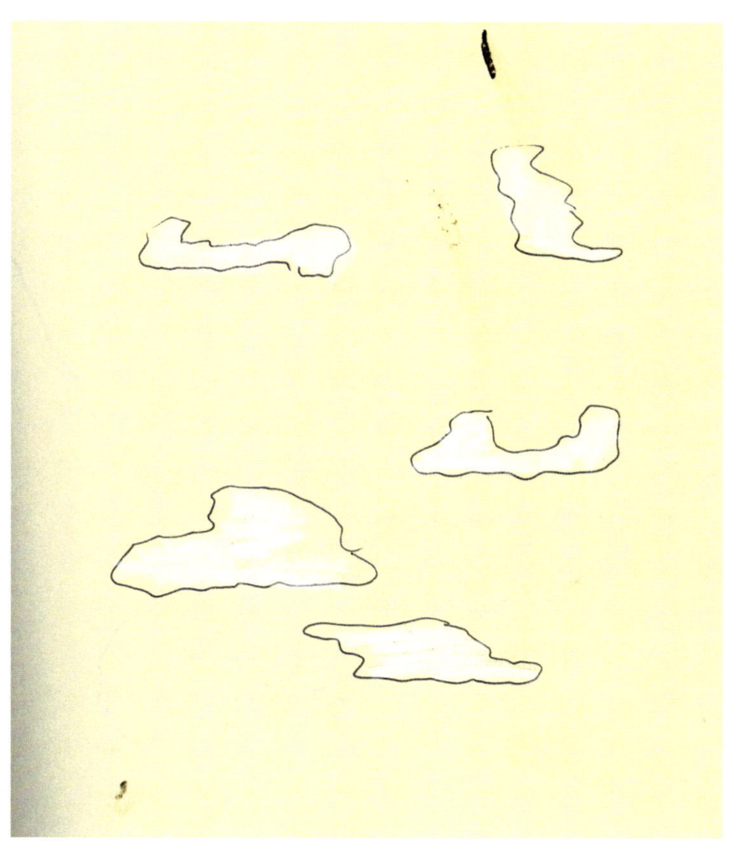

Nubes solis detritus sunt.

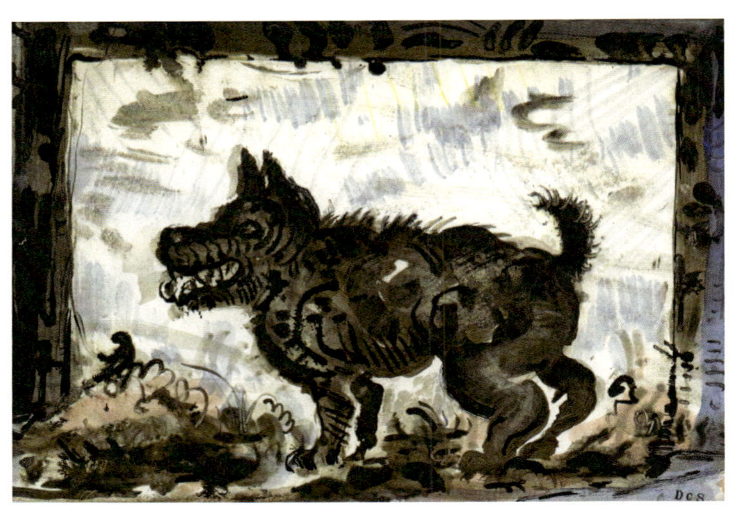

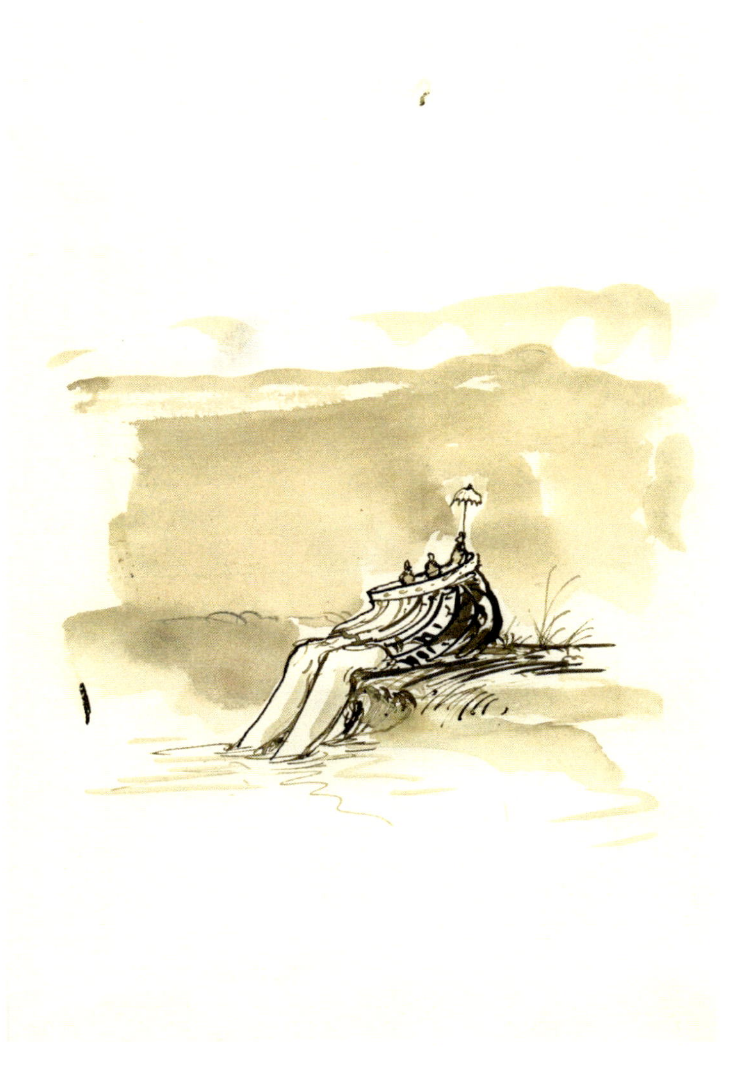

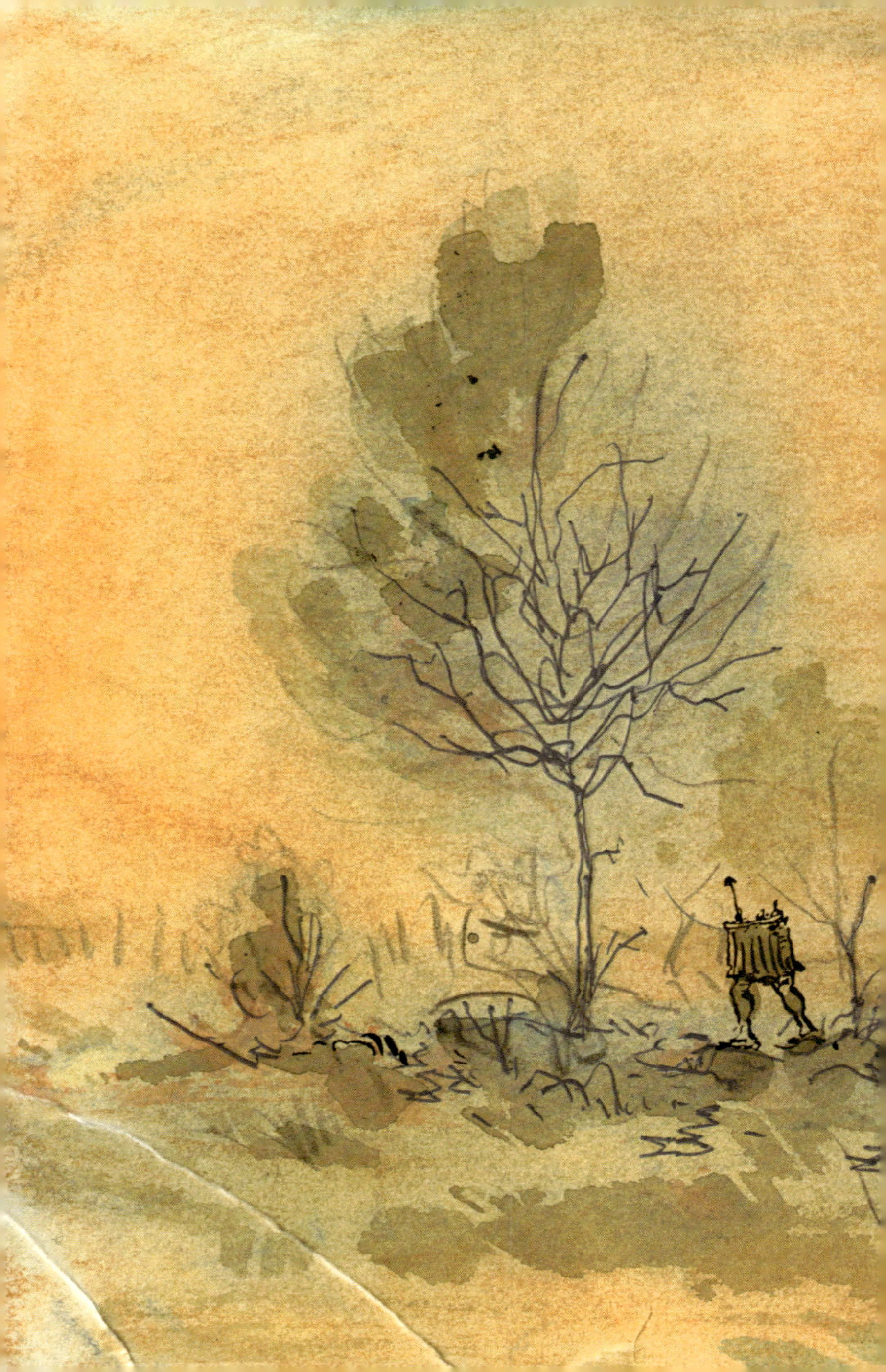

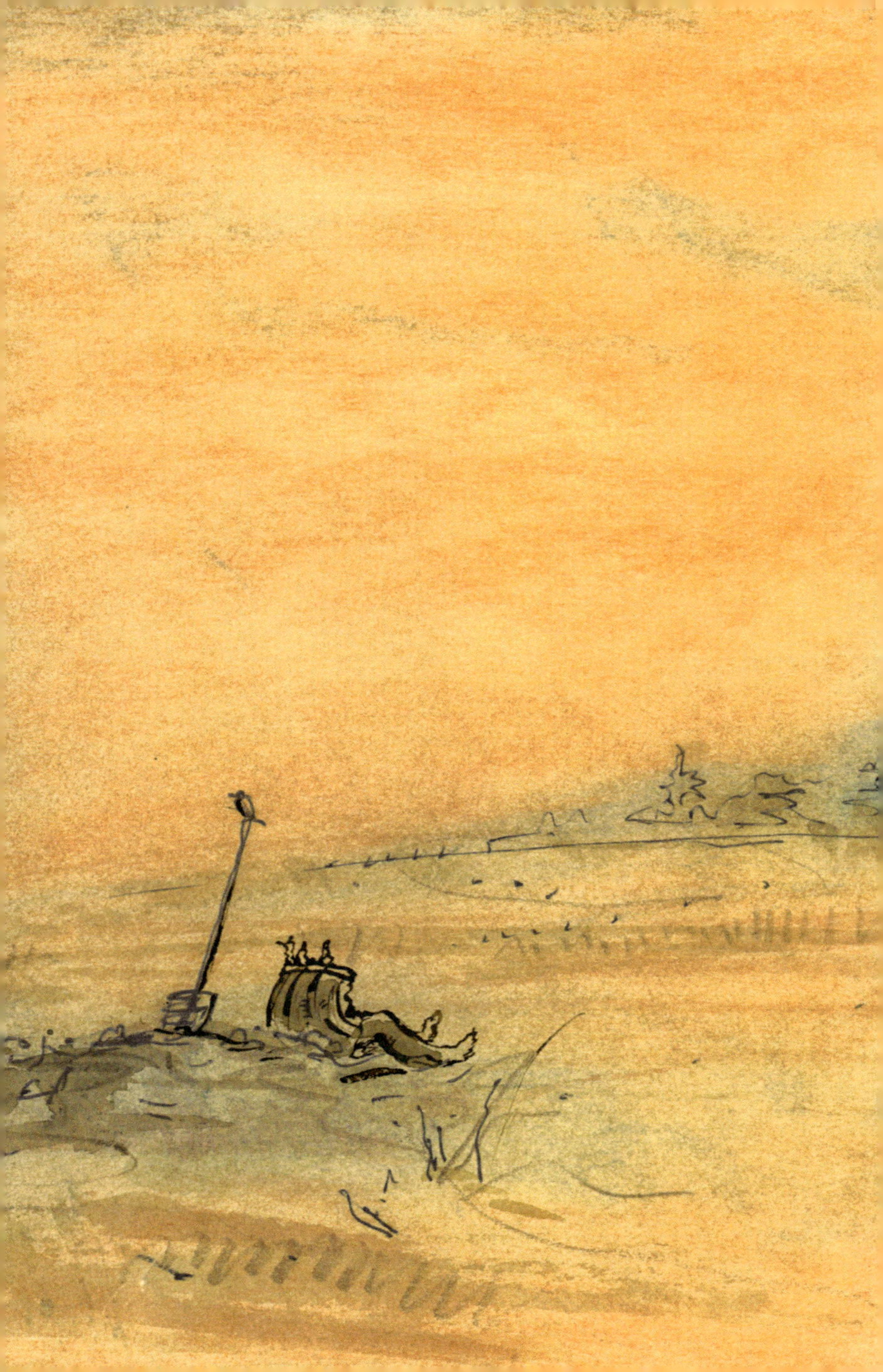

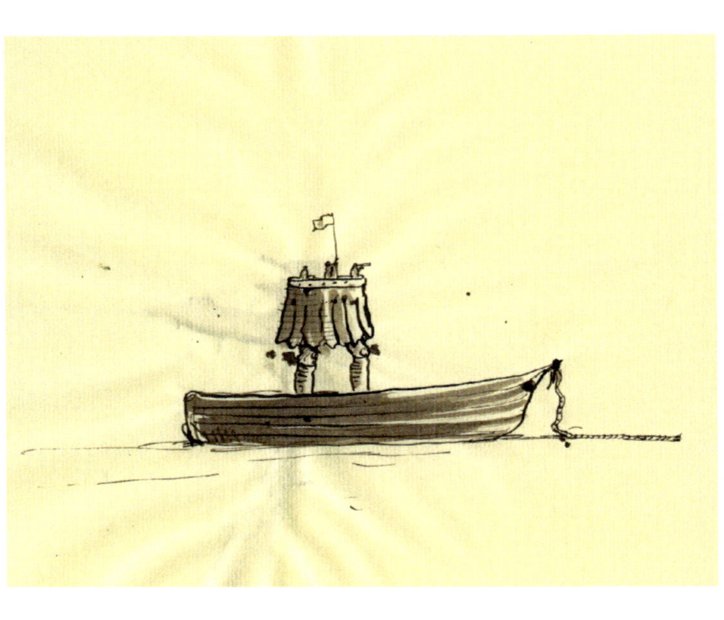

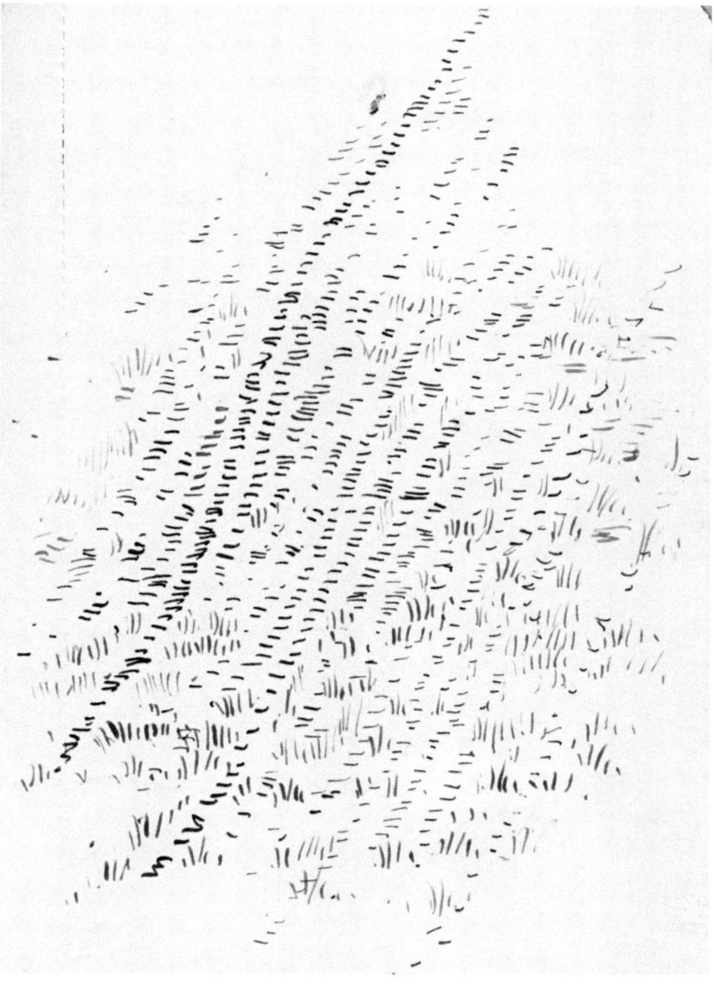

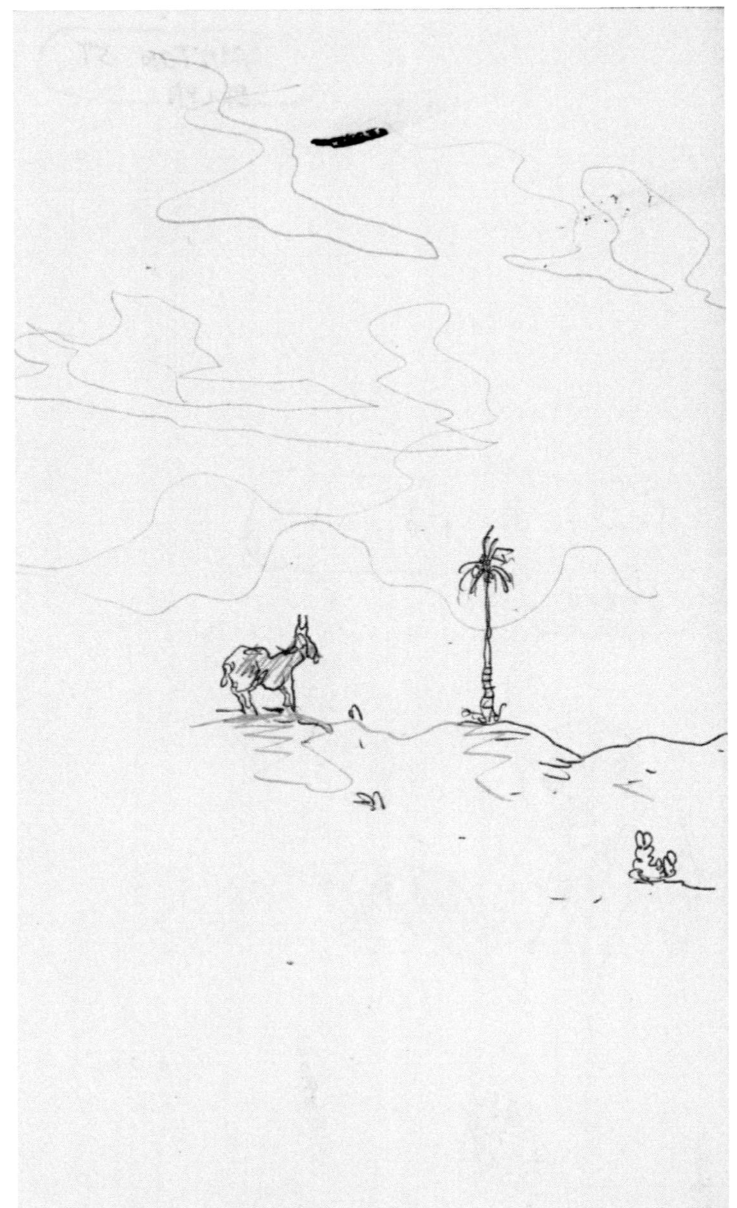

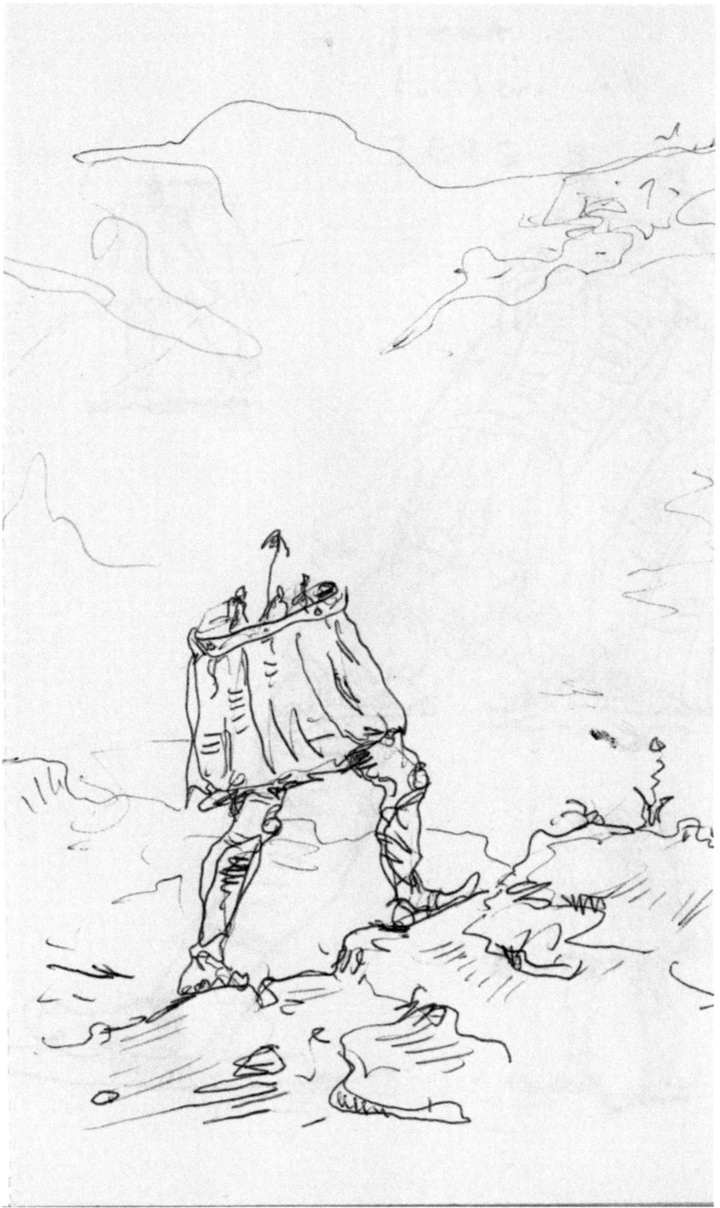

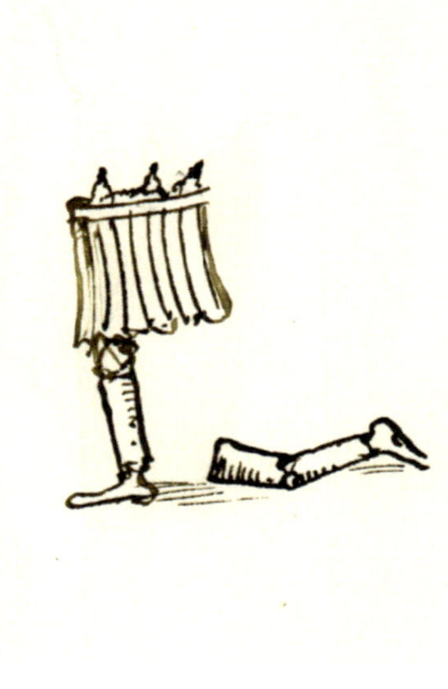

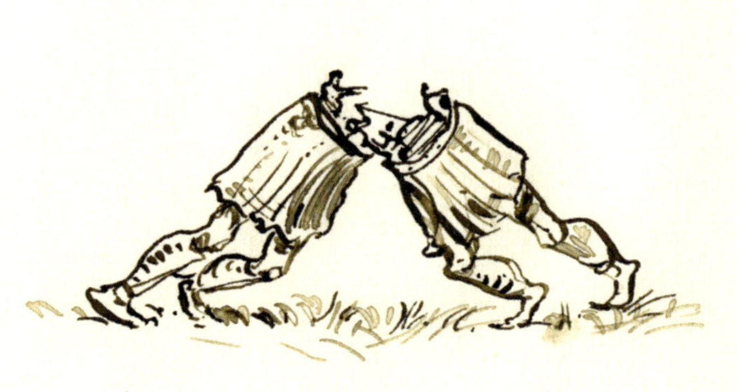

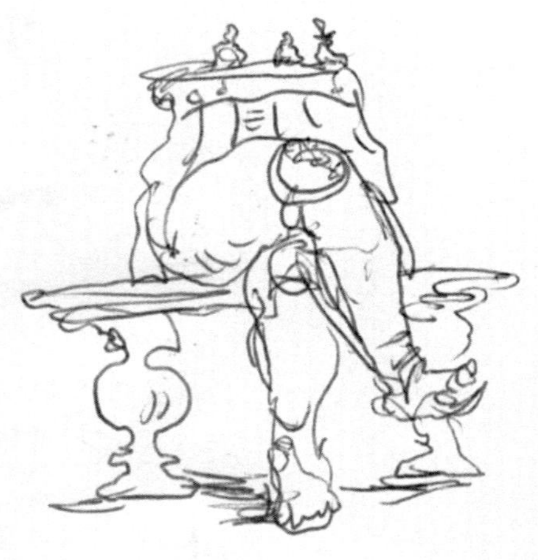

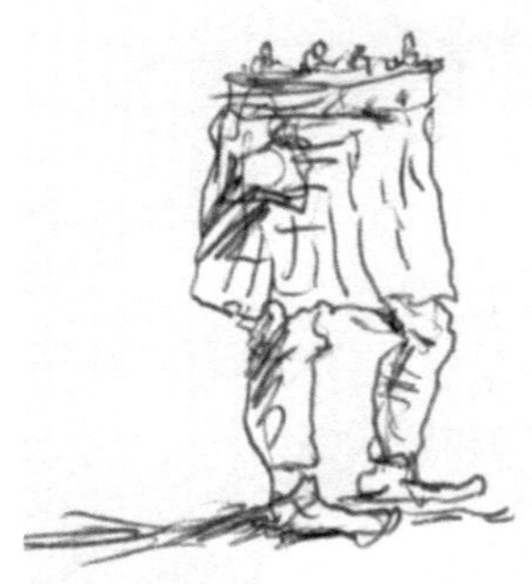

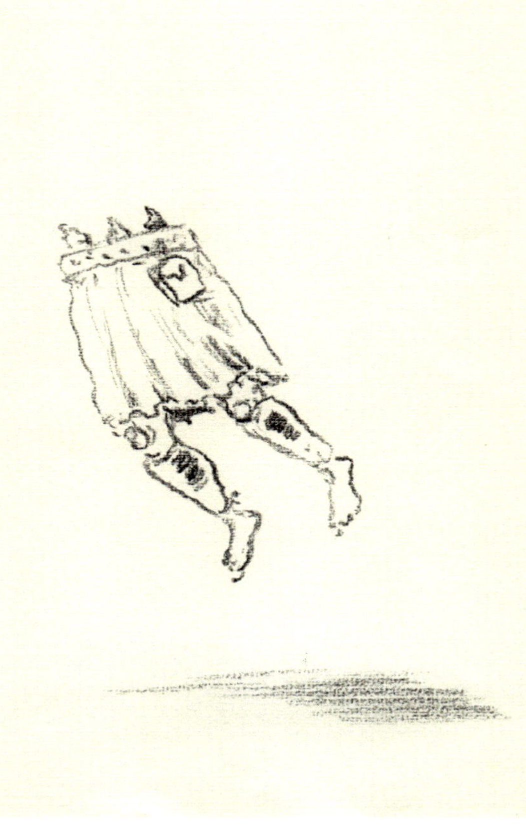

Saturday, 14 May 2016

10:50 AM *coffee cake, banana, coffee*
2:15 PM *brown-rice sushi with salmon and tuna, almonds*
4:12 PM *banana*
8:00 PM *black beans, cheese, avocado, corn chips, blueberries, water*

Sunday, 15 May 2016
2:10 AM *two cookies, water*
4:12 AM *blueberries, cookie, coffee*

Hail, Cretin!
David Scher

Design: Everything Studio, with assistance
from Sam Mason
Model: Michael Ballou
Assistance: Alan Fishbone, Kurt Hoffman,
Macha Tsarenkov, Brad Bolman, Ernie Mitchell
Editor: Sina Najafi

Cabinet Books wishes to thank the Andy Warhol
Foundation for the Visual Arts for its support of this
project.

ISBN: 978-1-932698-76-3
Printed by BookMobile, Minneapolis, USA

Published by Cabinet Books
Immaterial Incorporated
181 Wyckoff Street
Brooklyn, NY 11217 USA
<www.cabinetmagazine.org>
Copyright © 2016 David Scher and Immaterial
Incorporated.

Cabinet Books is the book imprint of Immaterial
Incorporated, a non-profit 501(c)3 organization whose
core activity is the publication of *Cabinet* magazine.